FOUNDATIONS OF MODERN HISTORY

General Editor A. GOODWIN
Formerly Professor of Modern History, University of Manchester

In the FOUNDATIONS OF MODERN HISTORY *Series*

I. R. Christie • *Crisis of Empire: Great Britain and the American Colonies 1754-1783*

J. R. Jones • *Britain and Europe in the Seventeenth Century*

R. F. Moore • *Liberalism and Indian Politics 1872-1922*

A. G. R. Smith • *The Government of Elizabethan England*

S. H. Steinberg • *The Thirty Years War and the Conflict for European Hegemony 1600-1660*

Gwyn A. Williams • *Artisans and Sans-Culottes: Popular Movements in France and Britain during the French Revolution*

Geoffrey B. A. M. Finlayson • *Decade of Reform: England in the Eighteen Thirties*

L. C. F. Turner • *Origins of the First World War*

Further titles to be announced

FOUNDATIONS OF MODERN HISTORY

Decade of Reform
England in the Eighteen Thirties

by GEOFFREY B. A. M. FINLAYSON
Lecturer in History, University of Glasgow

W·W·NORTON & COMPANY · INC·
NEW YORK

COPYRIGHT © 1970 BY GEOFFREY B. A. M. FINLAYSON

SBN 393 05406 3   (Cloth Edition)
SBN 393 09915 6   (Paper Edition)

Library of Congress Catalog Card No. 79-102943

PRINTED IN THE UNITED STATES OF AMERICA

1 2 3 4 5 6 7 8 9 0

General Preface

THIS series of short historical studies has as its main theme successive phases in the evolution of modern history from Renaissance times to the present day. Its general purpose is to provide within a limited compass, and at a reasonable cost, scholarly surveys of some of the fundamental developments which have influenced the civilisation and conditioned the outlook of the modern world. A second aim of the series will be to illustrate how not only the general direction of recent historical inquiry but also its very content and its relations with other disciplines have been progressively modified. If students of scientific or technological subjects who are extending their interests to the 'liberal' arts or social sciences are made aware of these trends something will have been done to close the gap between the scientific and humane cultures. A further feature of the series will be the endeavour to present selected periods of British history against the contemporary background of European development, with special emphasis on the nature and extent of cultural, scientific or intellectual interchange. Here the object will be to demonstrate the unity as well as the diversity of the European heritage and to re-examine its evolving significance in the context of global history.

The reason why the age of discontent and unrest in England after the Napoleonic wars was transformed, without revolution, into the age of Victorian 'Equipoise', must be sought in the intervening decade of reform in the 1830s. The most fundamental aspects of reform at that period were those which concerned the institutional fabric of the political and ecclesiastical Establishment, the administrative infra-structure of municipal government and the attitude of governments to the social and economic consequences of the Industrial Revolution. These are the leading themes studied in depth in the present volume by Mr. Finlayson.

How these reforms were achieved – whether as the result of the activity of parliamentary reformers or official committees of investigation, on the one hand, or at the instance of radical and popular pressure groups, on the other; the main phases of public controversy which they provoked; the response to them in different political or social environments in the capital and in the provinces; their immediate and more remote consequences in the constitutional, ecclesiastical and economic history of the period – these are the issues which the author elucidates in the light of his own researches and in relation to the work of other scholars.

In this way Mr. Finlayson is able to show how the great Reform Act of 1832 acted as a crucible of party development in the subsequent period and how it substantially altered the mutual relationships of the monarchy, the House of Lords and the House of Commons. The Municipal Corporations Act of 1835 not only established the elective principle in local borough government, but did so on terms which 'represented a much more immediate and substantial gain for the urban middle classes than the Reform Act had done'. Factory Reform in 1833 and Poor Law Reform in 1834 raised the whole issue of the desirability and extent of government intervention and one of the most interesting sections of the book is devoted to recent controversy on the growth of collectivism in an age which Dicey designated as one of 'Benthamite individualism'.

As most of these reforms, with the possible exception of the Municipal Corporations Act, aroused large-scale public controversy, compromise was an essential ingredient in their enactment and disillusionment with their practical results an inevitable consequence. In his final assessment, therefore, the author rightly emphasises not only the significance but the limitations of this decade of reform. These alienated the working class and only half satisfied the commercial and industrial entrepreneurs. The rise of Chartism and of the Anti-Corn Law League are thus seen as part of the response to the inadequacies of the reforms and the decline of the Parliamentary Radicals as yet another of their consequences.

A. GOODWIN

Author's Note

IN writing this short book I have been very conscious of the debt which I owe to the many historians who have worked and reflected on this period, and I only hope that I have done justice to their scholarship and opinions. To two such historians I should like to acknowledge a special debt, Mr. Michael G. Brock of Wolfson College, late of Corpus Christi College, Oxford, and Dr. James Tumelty of the University of Glasgow; by formal and informal ways, both have greatly stimulated and developed my interest in this decade of English history. In this connection, I should, perhaps, draw attention to the fact that the book is concerned with English rather than with British history. Since much of the reform legislation of the 1830s was different in application and effect in Scotland, it seemed best to exclude all but very occasional references to Scotland and to concentrate on England.

Finally, I should like to thank Mr. E. A. Hamilton and Miss Anne Jackson of Edward Arnold (Publishers) Ltd., for their assistance, Dr. Alan G. R. Smith of the University of Glasgow for his most helpful suggestions on reading the book in typescript and my wife for all that she has done towards its writing and completion.

University of Glasgow. August 1969.   G.B.A.M.F.

Abbreviations

The following abbreviations are used in footnotes

B.I.H.R.	*Bulletin of the Institute of Historical Research*
E.H.R.	*English Historical Review*
Ec.H.R.	*Economic History Review*
H.J.	*Historical Journal*
J.Ec.Hist.	*Journal of Economic History*
V.S.	*Victorian Studies*

Contents

Chapter   *Page*

GENERAL PREFACE   v

INTRODUCTION   1

1. REFORM: STATE AND CHURCH
    (i)   Reform of Parliament   5
    (ii) Reform of the Municipal Corporations; Church
         Reform   23
    (iii) Reform and Reformers in Decline   33

2. REFORM: GOVERNMENT AND SOCIETY
    (i)   Factory Reform   37
    (ii) Poor Law Reform   50
    (iii) The Scope and the Scale of Government   64

3. REFORM: THE RADICAL RESPONSE
    (i)   The Limitations of Reform   73
    (ii) Chartism and the Anti-Corn Law League   90
    (iii) The Demise of the Parliamentary Radicals   100

4. REFORM: THE LEGACY   104

SELECT BIBLIOGRAPHY   108

INDEX   113

For my wife, Elizabeth

Introduction

THE value of an historical study based on a number of years merely because they constitute a convenient or orthodox unit of time is always open to question. Centuries or decades may, indeed, signify little more than temporal divisions. But the 1830s in England have claims to be studied in their own right, not because they can be abstracted from the years which preceded and followed them, but because they have a unifying feature – that of reform – through which they may be studied. The reforms of the thirties might, indeed, be described almost year by year, and this, in itself, would provide an impressive record of achievement, and entitle the decade to be set beside other great reforming periods of English history, such as the 1880s, or the five or six years after 1906. But such an approach might degenerate into little more than a catalogue of legislation. Rather it may be more meaningful to consider the decade in the light of certain themes, all having reform at their centre, which offer a wider perspective than that afforded by a detailed study of every item of reforming legislation.

The first theme is that of reform in State and Church: and this deals with those measures which changed and adapted the country's political and ecclesiastical institutions. These had long been under attack on the grounds that they were corrupt, inefficient and took no account of changes in society. But with the exception of some minor alterations, they had remained untouched for centuries until the 1830s, when two major reforms affected England's political institutions: parliamentary reform in 1832 and municipal reform in 1835. In these two respects, then, the 'scythe of reform', as one radical put it, made inroads on the traditional preserves of the *ancien régime*, and political institutions were refashioned in recognition of the newly emerging forces in society; even if, especially in the case of parliamentary reform, little more than recognition was as yet given. Again the structure of the Church of England came under permanent review with the establishment of the Ecclesiastical Commission in 1836, the purpose of which was to propose reforming measures; and although the Church of England remained the Established Church, the cause of those who did not belong to it was to some degree advanced by the removal of certain disabilities on dissenters. These instalments of reform also raised the question of how far the process should be continued and extended; and in many respects this was the issue which dominated the politics of the thirties. There were those who felt that reform in State and Church should be far-reaching, both in character and the extent to which it should be carried; those who were prepared to envisage moderate and measured reform, but who did not see this as a continuing process; and yet again those who argued that reform was dangerous and disruptive and should be resisted. These broad categories, indeed, corresponded with the principal party divisions of the decade – Radical, Whig and Tory; and although the Tory point of view became more flexible than total resistance to reform with the development of the Conservative party in the mid-thirties, the function of the 'new' party was primarily to save established institutions from severe reforming encroachment by removing their worst defects. The provisions of the Reform Act and the development of parties in the decade, moreover, had considerable constitutional implications; they reacted on the distribution of power among King, Lords and Commons. In the course of the thirties, then, the political and ecclesiastical institutions of England underwent change and adaptation; the cause of new social groups was advanced; and in the process, issues were raised which affected the constitutional and political history of the decade.

The second theme of this book is concerned with measures which dealt with problems arising out of social conditions; in particular the conditions of children and young persons employed in factories, and also those of persons in receipt of poor relief. The large-scale growth of factories had been proceeding since at least the 1780s; and the social consequences of this aspect of industrialisation – the hours worked in factories and the environment in which they were worked – had attracted attention before the 1830s. The poor, of course, there had always been; and poor relief was a matter of long-standing concern. The system which existed at the beginning of the thirties was, indeed, basically that laid down in Elizabethan times, even if it had been considerably amended in the course of the centuries. But although neither factory reform nor poor law reform was new in the 1830s, both received extensive attention during the decade; and the solutions which were devised in the Factory Act of 1833 and the Poor Law Amendment Act of 1834 embodied certain features which were both novel in character and lasting in effect. Moreover, these measures, and others of a similar nature, raised the larger question of the scope and scale of government in society: the extent of government activity and the size of the government machine. Reform, then, is to be studied in these two aspects: political or institutional reform and social reform, along with the wider implications raised by each. The progress effected in these two directions during the thirties should, however, not be exaggerated. By the later years of the decade, political reform was virtually at a standstill and the party of resistance was steadily gaining ground at the expense of the party of reform. Social reform took place only within certain limits and its effects were by no means whole-heartedly appreciated by those whom it was meant to benefit.

This, therefore, leads on to the third theme of the book, which is concerned with the limitations of reform and more especially with the response of those who felt a sense of disappointment and frustration with the events of the decade. Here, reform is seen not 'from the top' as it tends to be in the first two themes, but 'from below'; from the point of view, not of politicians and civil servants at Westminster, but of radical and popular movements. By the end of the decade, it was indeed in these movements – then finally in the shape of Chartism and the Anti-Corn Law League – that the cause of reform was kept warm; a state of affairs which at once reflected the limitations of what had been achieved, and the discontent which such limitations had engendered.

By the end of the thirties it was the shortcomings of reform which were prominently displayed rather than its achievements. But the decade as a whole has claims to be regarded as of considerable long-term importance. It may, indeed, be argued that the reforms of the thirties started a process which has never wholly stopped, and which, in some respects, is still in progress. Further, certain political developments of the decade held importance for the future; and its radical and popular movements embraced ideas and tactics which later movements were to absorb and employ. Thus the final theme of the book traces what may be called the 'legacy of reform', both in the short-term problems which the decade left unsolved and in the long-term achievements which it bequeathed to later generations.

It must, of course, be said that this book leaves out almost as much as it includes. Many other reforms could be considered under the first two themes; and certain very important measures, such as legal reform and the abolition of slavery do not fit very well into either. The reader who, therefore, comes to the book expecting – in view of its title – the certain inclusion of a particular reform may well be disappointed; and this is regrettable. But, as has been said, the book is not intended to be a full survey of the reforms of the thirties and still less a comprehensive history of the decade; it is rather a commentary on it in the light of its most distinctive features.

CHAPTER ONE

Reform: State and Church

(i) Reform of Parliament

IN 1830, the issue of parliamentary reform was by no means new. The unreformed system of parliamentary representation had long been criticised from varying points of view and remedies put forward. An early approach to the question had been to advocate reform as a means of purging the constitution of corruption and restoring it to the 'purity' achieved at the time of the 'Glorious Revolution' of 1688; this was the approach of mid to late-eighteenth century reformers, who were men of substance and property. But in the 1790s, the English Jacobins, much influenced by Thomas Paine, made the cause more forward-looking, more democratic, and more popular in nature; and in the years after 1815, the prevalent social and economic distress convinced popular radicals that only an extensive reform of parliament could bring about an improvement in the material position of the working classes. This working class radical approach, democratic and demagogic in nature and tone, met with considerable resistance; it did not endear the cause to other sections of society, and in the war and post-war period, the propertied classes found themselves on the side of order and stability. Nevertheless, by the 1820s the cause of reform was winning its recruits among these propertied classes, even if their grievances and aspirations were rather different from those of working class radicals. Here the criticism of the unreformed system was that it failed to afford sufficient recognition, not to the poor, but to the newly rich. Manufacturers and industrialists of midland and northern towns resented the fact that the 'political nation' did not embrace their thriving communities, but did embrace tiny rural villages with a handful of voters; and they were coming to feel that their business and economic interests could not be adequately fostered by a parliament which, even if it had certain 'manufacturing' representatives in it, still gave overwhelming preponderance to agricultural and aristocratic interests. Thus the struggle for parliamentary reform was joined by adherents of what may broadly be called 'middle class' or 'business men's' radicalism, who sought not universal suffrage, but sufficient political power to match their economic power. Then there was a third approach to the question, which derived not so much from a material interest as from an intellectual commitment. This was the approach of the philosophical or 'parliamentary' radicals, the 'intellectuals in politics' as they have been called,[1] who owed many of their ideas to Jeremy Bentham and James Mill. Their attitude to reform was to see it not so much in the context of furthering any sectional interest, but rather as a weapon with which to reduce the power of the 'aristocracy' and increase that of the 'people'; even if it should be added that both of these terms had, for them, an abstract rather than an actual meaning.[2] Thus for long before 1830 parliamentary reform in various guises had a wide appeal to that amorphous conglomeration known as the radical movement, which may be divided into the categories suggested only in a broad and general manner.

Reform, moreover, was not without its parliamentary sponsors, even in the unreformed parliament. It was not official Whig policy, but individual Whigs, in particular Lord John Russell, became closely associated with it. His approach was directed towards removing some of the most glaring abuses of the old system. Thus in 1827–28 Russell urged the disfranchisement of two blatantly corrupt boroughs, Penryn and East Retford, and the transfer of their seats to Manchester and Birmingham. This was an approach which was admittedly limited in nature; Russell was, as it were, tinkering with the existing system. His schemes stopped far short of the ideas of working class and parliamentary radicals. But they had something in common with the views of middle class radicals, and indeed, one of Russell's arguments in introducing his measures was the inadequate representation which the unreformed system afforded to industry and commerce.

Yet, although parliamentary reform had long been advocated, the question assumed a new urgency in the years immediately before 1830. In the late 1820s there was a marked increase in the activity and organisation of the radical movement in the country.

[1] J. Hamburger, *Intellectuals in Politics. John Stuart Mill and the Philosophic Radicals* (New Haven, 1965).

[2] *Ibid.*, pp. 53–6. This point has received critical attention from R. S. Neale, 'Class and Class Consciousness in Early Nineteenth Century England: Three Classes or Five?' *V.S.*, xii, September 1968, 5–32.

A trade and business recession and a number of bad harvests brought with them hardship and unrest; and these in turn provoked a clamour for redress and remedy. Various remedies were canvassed: a reform of the system of currency, a rigid adoption of economy, the abolition of pensions and sinecures. But a common assumption was that some measure of parliamentary reform was a necessary preliminary to the achievement of these remedies: the indispensable prelude to any effective change. In these circumstances, it proved possible to effect some kind of union between working class and middle class radical views, especially where, as in Birmingham, the structure of society and industry was conducive to such a development.[1]

Thus in 1830, the Birmingham Political Union was set up at the instigation of Thomas Attwood, a banker, 'to obtain by every just and legal means such a reform in the Commons House of Parliament as may ensure a real and effectual representation of the lower and middle classes of the people in that House'. The Union pointed out that whereas the Church, Law and the landed and monied interests were all represented, 'the interests of industry and trade had scarcely any representatives at all.' Attwood himself saw a relaxation of the currency system as the solution to the distress of the country, but allegiance to this was not a condition of membership of the Union. The Birmingham example was discussed elsewhere, and by the end of 1830 had been followed in many other towns, such as Liverpool and Newcastle. It is true that this aim to unite 'the middle and lower classes' did not appeal to the whole radical movement, and was not by any means universally achieved. In certain places, such as Leeds and Manchester, working class unions were found alongside and separate from middle class unions;[2] and there remained a distinct distrust of co-operation with the middle classes among those working class radicals who, in 1831, formed themselves into the National Union of the Working Classes and met at the Rotunda in London. As ever, the radical movement presented no united front. Nevertheless, by 1830, the general aim of parliamentary reform commanded wide acceptance, even if there were differences of opinion as to its nature and purpose. Certainly the growth of the Political Unions indicated a degree of activity and organisation which had

[1] A. Briggs, 'The Background of the Parliamentary Reform Movement in Three English Cities (1830–32)', *Cambridge Historical Journal* x, 297–302.

[2] *Ibid.*, 302–15.

been lacking in previous years. Further, their existence gave parliamentary radicals like Francis Place and Joseph Parkes material on which to exercise their talents for political manipulation, and a means of persuading the governing classes that reform was necessary in order to prevent large-scale disturbance or even revolution.[1]

In 1829–30, the issue of reform acquired a new immediacy not only in radical but also in parliamentary circles. The only success gained by Lord John Russell in the 1820s had been the disfranchisement of the borough of Grampound; and even then, his proposal that the seats made available should be given to Leeds was defeated. A county was thought to be a safer recipient of the seats than a new borough; and the representation of Yorkshire was accordingly strengthened. Parliamentary reform, then, made little headway. The Whigs remained out of office, and 'liberal Toryism' in the 1820s stopped short of applying 'liberal' principles to institutions. Nevertheless, various developments in the political and parliamentary situation in the late 1820s combined to bring the issue of reform into prominence. The passing of Catholic Emancipation by the Wellington government in 1829 made some Whigs hopeful that the Duke might follow up the measure by a moderate reform of parliament. But of greater significance was the disintegrating effect which Catholic Emancipation had on the Tory party, and the fact that it made certain ultra-Tories espouse the cause of reform. In their eyes, the sponsoring of Catholic Emancipation by the Wellington ministry, and even more, the way in which it passed parliament, provided evidence of such corruption and patronage at the disposal of the government as to make parliamentary reform necessary to purge the political system. Again, such purging would reduce the possibility that Catholics might, after Emancipation, secure parliamentary representation by way of the nomination boroughs. Further, certain county members and ultra-Tories – what has been called the 'country party'[2] – had other grievances against the Wellington ministry. They were alienated by its failure to take any positive action over the distress of the late 1820s, which affected rural areas as well as urban; or to make any changes in the system of currency which they held partly responsible for the trouble. Such grievances

[1] J. Hamburger, *James Mill and the Art of Revolution* (New Haven, 1963), *passim*.

[2] D. C. Moore, 'The Other Face of Reform', *V.S.*, v, 7–34.

led this 'country party' to see reform as a means of redress; an approach which had something in common with that of the radical movement, although there was a wide gulf in underlying political attitudes.

Reform thus came into greater prominence in parliamentary circles in the years immediately before 1830; and the process was taken further by the General Election made necessary by the death of George IV in June 1830, and held in July and August of that year. As we have seen, reform, as sponsored by the radicals, Whigs or members of the 'country party', already commanded wide interest; it did not require news of the July Revolution in France to spark off reforming sentiment at the elections, most of which had, in fact, been held before that news arrived.[1] It would be an over-simplification to suggest that the elections returned a great 'reforming' majority; in the new parliament the political situation was far from clear-cut. Nevertheless, reform was one issue which could scarcely be avoided by the returning Wellington ministry, if it was to gain enough support in the House to remain in office. Yet the famous speech of the Duke in November 1830, in which he claimed that the existing state of representation enjoyed the 'full and entire confidence of the country', and refused to countenance any measure of reform, made it clear that the issue was indeed to be evaded by the ministry. It is possible that Wellington may have felt that the recent association of reform with radical agitation and 'foreign' revolution had cured the 'country party' of any ideas on the subject; and that his strong anti-reform speech was designed to bolster his precarious parliamentary position by rallying his recent critics back to his side. Some ultras did, indeed, return; but the Duke's handling of the situation, if designed to strengthen his ministry, did not do so.[2] On the contrary, it contributed to a union of parliamentary opponents which made it impossible for him to control the House, as was made evident by the defeat of the ministry on a Civil List motion some days later. At this, the Duke resigned; and although the incoming ministry under Grey may be more correctly described as an amalgam of most of the Duke's parliamentary opponents than a strictly 'Whig' ministry, it came into office on the basis that

[1] N. Gash, 'English Reform and French Revolution in the General Election of 1830', in R. Pares and A. J. P. Taylor (eds.), *Essays Presented to Sir Lewis Namier* (1956), pp. 258–88.

[2] D. C. Moore, *op. cit.*, 25–6.

parliamentary reform would be introduced.

In 1830, then, reform commanded support in the country and
there was a ministry in office committed to its pursuit. This is not,
of course, to say that the new 'Whig' ministry was at all in sympathy with every aspect of the radical movement. The ministry
was highly aristocratic in composition and 'orthodox' in its social
attitudes. Certain members of the government, for example
Russell and Durham, viewed parts of the reform movement with
some favour, although not its more extreme working class
elements. Grey, however, was less well disposed to the movement
as a whole, and regarded the Political Unions with suspicion.
'We did not cause the excitement about Reform,' he told the King.
'We found it in full vigour when we came into office.' Nevertheless, even to Grey, the fact that excitement on the subject existed
was inescapable if unpalatable; thus to the long-standing Whig
inclination towards parliamentary reform was added the belief
that in the circumstances of 1830, reform was expedient and
necessary. This would remove the worst features of the old system
and redress its most glaring anomalies. It would disfranchise the
most notorious of the nomination boroughs and bring within the
political nation at least some of the hitherto unrepresented areas;
but it would strengthen the position of those areas previously
under-represented, such as the counties. It would also enfranchise
the propertied and more respectable contenders for the parliamentary vote. And all this, it was hoped, would be sufficient to
satisfy at least part of the radical movement, to end the popular
agitation and to bring about a final settlement of the question.
Such were the broad principles behind the Reform Bill introduced by Russell in March 1831. The Whigs, it has been said,
were 'convinced that their task was essentially conservative, a
rescue operation on behalf of rank and property'.[1]

The bill did not by any means commend itself to all parts of the
radical movement and was fiercely denounced by its more extreme
elements. But it was reasonably well received by the Political
Unions, which now looked upon the Whigs as their parliamentary
champions, however unwilling the Whigs to be cast in this role.
The bill, however, had not only to stand the test of the radical
movement; it also had to stand the test of Parliament, in its full
sense of King, Lords and Commons. And here difficulties arose.
William IV, unlike his predecessor George IV was not opposed to

[1] D. Southgate, *The Passing of the Whigs, 1832–1886* (1962), p. 21.

reform in principle, but when it became clear that it could not pass the Commons and Lords with the ease which he had expected, he became increasingly hesitant and obstructive. And it became amply clear that reform would not, indeed, pass easily in the light of the vigorous parliamentary opposition with which the Whig proposals were met. They were too extreme for many former Tory supporters of reform; and although the 'Tory' point of view, like the 'Whig' covered different shades of opinion, it came to be almost wholly agreed that reform, as proposed by the Whigs, was dangerous and destructive. It would upset the balance of the constitution; it would lead to social revolution; and despite the Whig assurances, it could not be final, but was bound to lead to further and more extensive reform. Such views were expressed forcibly by the Tories in both Houses, if most forcibly by the ultras in the Lords; and their opposition, along with its effect on the King, made the Whigs' task of getting reform through parliament a long and arduous one.[1]

The efforts of the Whig government may, therefore, be seen in the context of the activity of the popular forces in the country and that of the parliamentary processes at Westminster; the one expressing broad support for their proposals, and the other presenting obstacles and difficulties. Three episodes between the introduction of the first Reform Bill in March 1831, and the passage of the third bill in June 1832 were of particular relevance to this dual context; and each raised points of constitutional importance. The first was after the Whigs had been defeated in committee on the bill in the Commons, and when a dissolution of parliament and General Election had followed in April–May 1831. The bill had indeed passed its second reading in the Commons by only one vote; and in the light of this parliamentary opposition, Grey had contemplated a dissolution for some time. Grey felt that a dissolution was necessary if the popular excitement over reform were to be kept directed to the Whig bill, which he regarded as a 'safe and legitimate object'. A dissolution would channel that excitement to the support of the King's Government; but if other steps were taken, popular attention might be directed elsewhere, and the situation in the country assume more menacing proportions. The proposed dissolution and election were, however, strongly opposed by the King; he had fears as he told Grey,

[1] The fullest account is to be found in J. R. M. Butler, *The Passing of the Great Reform Bill* (1914).

that an election would result in the country 'being thrown into convulsion from the Land's End to John O'Groats House'. Further, on the actual defeat, the traditional constitutional practice for the ministry would have been to resign, leaving the King to form a new ministry; and if the dissolution cut across this practice, it also involved an appeal to the electorate, more or less on a single issue, over and against the legislature. This was much criticised as usurping the deliberative function of the Commons and raised fears of rule by delegates and demagogues. Such fears were, of course, exaggerated; but the whole episode appeared to highlight the popular forces and to cast the parliamentary processes into the shade.

Much the same kind of issue was raised in the second episode under consideration. This was between October and December 1831, when loud popular reaction greeted the rejection by the Lords of a second bill – little different from the first – which had been introduced by Russell in July, and had passed the Commons in September. On the Lords' rejection of this bill in October, the Birmingham Political Union made vigorous protests, and there were riots in Derby, Nottingham and Bristol. The National Political Union was formed in an attempt to harness the various energies of all classes to reform. Place and Parkes were especially busy, pointing out the dangers of the popular demand being disappointed. The precise importance of this outside pressure and persuasion is difficult to measure with any certainty; the Whigs were not the puppets of the popular movement. Yet, their decision not to resign, and to introduce a bill substantially the same as that rejected by the Lords, owed at least something to their fears that a much diluted measure might dangerously provoke the popular movement;[1] once more, the best course was to keep as far as possible to a bill which was 'safe and legitimate', but which would also calm the popular agitation and, indeed, put an end to it. Thus a third bill, 'no less efficient' than that rejected by the Lords, was introduced in December 1831. Again, however, this involved rejecting the advice of the King, who did his best to persuade Grey to settle the dispute between the Houses by coming to terms with the Lords with a 'diluted' compromise measure; and it involved ignoring the views and powers of the House of Lords. In the eyes of many critics, the implications of this episode were even

[1] H. Ferguson, 'The Birmingham Political Union and the Government', *V.S.*, iii, 271, 275.

more dangerous than those of the first, since it was now not the
electorate but the Political Unions, bodies outside the formal
limits of the constitution, which were involved; the Whigs were,
indeed, accused of being in league with the unconstitutional
forces of the country to coerce the constitutional. Again, this was
exaggerated; but again the episode served to emphasise the popular background to reform.

The third episode in question also witnessed the popular elements in the situation ranged against the parliamentary. This was
in May–June 1832 when a Tory amendment to the third bill was
carried in committee in the Lords against Grey's wishes, and the
King accepted the resignation of the Whigs rather than create
enough peers to force the bill through the Lords. Even although a
Tory ministry would now have been compelled to introduce some
measure of reform, Wellington's attempt to form such a ministry
was made to the accompaniment of protests from the Birmingham
Political Union and plans for an insurrection, a refusal to pay
taxes and a run on the bank; the slogan was coined, 'To Stop the
Duke Go for Gold.' Further, the failure of Wellington to form an
administration, and the return of the Whigs with the written
assurance of the King that peers would be created to pass the
reform was greeted with jubilation. Once again, there was talk of
the unconstitutional forces of the country coercing the constitutional. In fact, it is open to question how far the popular
movement did affect Wellington's failure and dictate the return
of the Whigs.[1] Some Tory members may, indeed, have been afraid
of the popular consequences of a Tory ministry being formed;
but another explanation was the unwillingness of many Tories to
join a ministry which would sponsor a reform to which they had
been so bitterly opposed. This was the attitude of Peel; and without Peel, the Duke's task was virtually hopeless. Yet the popular
aspects of the question had once again been highlighted; and even
if they were less influential on this occasion than on the others, it
remains true that the established parts of the constitution had
again suffered defeat. The King was forced to take back a
ministry whose resignation he had accepted, and to give that
ministry the firm assurance which he had previously refused; and
the Lords only evaded the indignity of a creation of peers by
dropping their resistance.

The three episodes which have been considered do not, of

[1] *Ibid.*, 272–5.

course, provide anything approaching a full history of the passing of the Reform Bill; and the particular aspect which they illustrate is by no means the only aspect of the question. Further, even concentrating on 'popular pressure' and 'parliamentary resistance', certain additional points may be made. It is, for example, difficult to establish how strong the 'popular pressure' was. If it is suggested that fear of revolution affected the movements of politicians in the struggle, it remains uncertain how important a part this played;[1] the activities of the Whigs cannot be explained in terms of this consideration alone. And, as we have seen, the same kind of qualification is also necessary with regard to the episode of May–June 1832 which involved the Tories. Further, the established parts of the constitution which put up resistance did not emerge from the struggle quite so crushed as might be thought. The institution which had been most completely coerced was the House of Lords, but this did not mean that the Lords had no future role; within a few years, indeed, their Lordships were showing marked signs of life. Yet even allowing for all these qualifications, it remains true that the struggle over the bill did witness the existence of popular opinion and agitation on a considerable scale and in an organised form; and the manner of the bill's passing showed that, given such popular pressure, the established parts of the constitution, however unbending, could not but take account of it.

If the passing of the Reform Bill brought popular and 'unrepresented' opinion in the country into prominence, one of the effects of the Act was to bring within the political nation new and hitherto unrepresented areas, interests and voters. Of the one hundred and forty-three seats made available for redistribution by total or partial disfranchisement, sixty-five were given to boroughs previously unrepresented; thus urban centres of population and importance were granted political recognition at the expense of the worst of the rotten and nomination boroughs. After 1832, sixty-four English boroughs had electorates of over 1,000, and of these, twenty-nine had more than 2,000 voters on the roll.[2] This process helped to redress some of the geographical anomalies of the old system; the north and midlands of England gained representation as the south lost it, and the representation of London, which had previously suffered against both north and

[1] J. Hamburger, *James Mill and the Art of Revolution*, p. 271 ff.

[2] N. Gash, *Politics in the Age of Peel* (1953), p. 76.

south, was increased. All this meant the disappearance from the electoral map of places like Old Sarum, Bramber, and Plympton; and the appearance of boroughs like Leeds, Manchester, Birmingham, and, in London, Finsbury and Tower Hamlets. Further, many of the newly enfranchised boroughs were considered to represent the manufacturing and commercial interests of the country, which thus found a place within the political nation. As far as the new borough franchise was concerned, the £10 householder qualification was a uniform one, but it could have different effects in different places; the nature of a £10 house varied from borough to borough, and £10 was only the bottom of the scale. As a generalisation subject to local variation, however, it may be said that this particular qualification enfranchised the majority of the middle classes living in the boroughs represented after 1832,[1] although it excluded the bulk of the working classes. In some respects, then, the Reform Act marked an adjustment of the electoral system to take account of urban, industrial 'modern' England.

Yet, even considering only the borough representation after 1832, this kind of judgment may give a very partial impression if it is left unqualified. For such new aspects of the electoral structure must be set in the context of the whole structure after the Reform Act if they are not to appear out of proportion. It is true that new populous boroughs were for the first time represented; but it is also true that many older, smaller and indeed semi-rural boroughs continued to be represented. It was, in fact, a minority of English boroughs represented after 1832 which had over 2,000 or even 1,000 voters. One hundred and twenty-three had under 1,000 voters; of these, ninety-two had between 300 and 1,000 voters and thirty-one had fewer than 300.[2] Again, the former over-representation of the south of England against the north, although lessened, remained after 1832; and the representation of London still did not keep pace even with that of the north of England. Further, if the enfranchisement of new boroughs recognised new interests in the country, the survival of so many small boroughs and of open voting, which the Reform Act did not alter, meant the continuing political existence of many older and private interests. This might be the influence of a local family, a member of which would almost invariably be returned for a particular

[1] *Ibid.*, p. 100.

[2] *Ibid.*, p. 77.

borough for a variety of reasons: economic influence, social position, personal popularity. And there were still after 1832 'proprietary' boroughs, where the voters would return any nominee of the patron, and not necessarily only a member of a local family; or again, the prevailing interest might be that of an institution such as a University, as at Cambridge, or a municipal corporation, with funds or charitable bequests at its disposal to 'influence' voters.[1] The electoral system after 1832, as far as the boroughs were concerned, thus still allowed considerable scope for the expression of private interests, many of which derived from aristocratic and landed sources. While conceding, then, that the Reform Act enfranchised voters who may be broadly described as middle class, it must be borne in mind that influence could still be brought to bear through the borough representation on behalf of the older established, landed classes.

Furthermore, the pool of seats available for re-distribution was used not only to enfranchise hitherto unrepresented boroughs, but also to increase the representation of the counties. Sixty-five additional seats were granted to the counties of England and Wales. It is true that in terms of numbers of voters and seats, the counties after the Reform Act remained under-represented compared with the boroughs; but in terms of the representation of interests, which was much more the contemporary concern, the increase in county seats was considered to strengthen the landed interest. With regard to the county voters, the continuing existence after 1832 of the forty-shilling freeholder meant the predominance in most counties of a voter who had always enjoyed a measure of political independence, since his franchise derived from the possession of property; and the fact that this property might be of different kinds meant that the forty-shilling freeholder could belong to various social groups. Nevertheless, despite this tendency to independence and social diversity, in the majority of cases the forty-shilling freeholder had always been subject to the social environment of the counties in which the landed classes held all the public offices and were the 'natural leaders' of society; and the Reform Act did very little to change this situation, or the sense of deference and obligation which it induced. It may, indeed, be argued that the Act reinforced the landed interest in the counties. For one thing, it withdrew from the counties those voters who, after 1832, qualified for both a

[1] *Ibid.*, Chapters 7, 8, 9.

county and a borough franchise; such voters had to vote in the borough, and this may be regarded as having reduced the urban element in the counties. Moreover, the Act created three new county franchises, two of which, the copyhold and the leasehold qualifications, involved the possession of land; and the third – the result of the 'Chandos clause' of the Act – clearly provided an opportunity for landlord influence by enfranchising the tenant farmer who paid a rental of £50 yearly. Taking account of all these points, it can be seen that the landed interest and the landed classes emerged from the Reform Act with very considerable strength.

If, then, the electoral system after 1832 recognised new elements in the country and society, these had to exist within a framework which still gave great scope to many of the older elements. Moreover, before a man could stand for parliament, he had to possess a certain amount of property, and until 1838, only landed property could be counted. In practice, this property qualification was often evaded, but this did not mean that possession of property was unnecessary to get into parliament. Such was the electoral system and the electoral practices of the time that property was very necessary; it might be the property – and the influence which went with it – of a family or landowner, or the candidate's own property and wealth needed to meet electoral expenses. These expenses could often be enormous since the Reform Act did nothing to limit them; and with open voting, almost every contested election, in new constituencies as in old, was accompanied by bribery and corruption on a very considerable scale. And even if a man were elected reasonably cheaply, there was no payment for being a member of parliament: the member had to live at his own expense throughout a parliament which might sit for seven years.

It is not, therefore, very surprising that the social composition of parliament was not greatly altered by the Reform Act.[1] It is true that there were lawyers, merchants and manufacturers in parliament after 1832; but there had always been a sprinkling of members from such trades and professions. By far the largest group in the House of Commons after 1832, and for many years thereafter, was drawn from the landowning classes; between 1833 and 1867, well over half the members of the House were connected with land. And if the aristocratic and landed interest continued to

[1] S. F. Wooley, 'The Personnel of the Parliament of 1833', *E.H.R.*, liii, 240–62

dominate the House of Commons, this was even more true of the Cabinet. In none of the mid-nineteenth century cabinets was the landed interest in a minority. Thus Walter Bagehot writing in 1859 could say 'The series of Cabinet Ministers presents a nearly unbroken rank of persons who either are themselves large land-owners, or are connected closely by birth or inter-marriage with large landowners'.[1]

When, therefore, the dust had settled and what had been achieved was clearly seen, it was evident that the Act had done little to shake the dominance of the established interests and classes. For the most part, it left the working classes outside the political nation altogether. It was not the numbers of the country which were granted political recognition in 1832 but the interests; the population of England in 1831 was some thirteen millions, of which one in five adult males had the vote as a result of the Reform Act. And if the Act advanced the cause of the manu-facturing, middle class interest, it by no means raised it to the point where it exercised political domination; the share of power granted to it in 1832 was very much that of a junior partner.

Nevertheless, just as the manner of the bill's passing had reacted on the established parts of the constitution, the Act itself, and the issues which it raised, were not without their effects in this same connection. The Crown had emerged rather unhappily from the Reform Bill crisis, and it cannot be said that the Act helped its fortunes. Rather, it assisted the decline which had been proceed-ing since the onset of economical reforms in the 1780s had reduced much of the political patronage at the Crown's disposal. By disfranchising the nomination boroughs, many of which had been controlled in the government interest, the Act removed a former source of electoral and parliamentary support for a ministry of the King's choice. The effect of this should not be exaggerated, for the ability of the Crown to 'make a House' had already virtually disappeared; but the nomination boroughs had proved a very useful mode of re-entry to the Commons for a member who, by the convention of the times, had to seek re-election to the House on his appointment to office.[2] The loss of the nomination boroughs, then, meant the disappearance of one of the assets

---

[1] Quoted in G. Kitson Clark, *The Making of Victorian England* (1962), pp. 209-10.

[2] N. Gash, *Reaction and Reconstruction in English Politics, 1832-52* (Oxford, 1965), pp. 3-4.

which the Crown had still been able to put at the disposal of its ministers. Further, the Act contributed to the growth of local party associations in the constituencies by its requirement that all voters had to be registered; this was exploited in a party interest by local committees set up to encourage supporters to register, to challenge the qualifications of opponents and to secure their removal from the register. The Tories were first in the field here with F. R. Bonham as their leading expert;[1] but the Whigs, if some way behind, did not neglect this early aspect of party organisation. Further, there were the beginnings of central party organisation with the establishment of the Tory Carlton Club in 1832 and the Whig Reform Club in 1836; both clubs were political in nature and tended to be the centres of party gossip and information about constituencies, registration and candidates. Such early forms of party organisation did not in any way mean the arrival of highly disciplined parties; the electoral system after 1832 left room for too many private and personal influences for party to be all-pervasive. Yet these may be said to have reflected and, indeed, engendered a measure of party spirit; and this spirit, evident in post-Reform Bill politics and deriving in part from the question of how far reform should be carried, cut across the old idea that the monarch could appoint ministers of his choice, who would be willing to work together, and would be supported out of a common loyalty and sense of public duty.

The electoral system and political situation after 1832 thus reduced the area of initiative for the Crown, as, indeed, William IV was soon to learn.[2] The Whigs had returned to office with a great majority after the first General Election under the reformed system held in December 1832; and William, fearful that they might press on to further reform, became increasingly anxious to replace the ministry by a coalition which would act in the conservative interest. In a sense, he sought a return to the old idea of a 'broad bottomed' ministry, and on the retirement of the Whig leader, Grey, in 1834, attempted to bring this about. Melbourne, Grey's successor, was asked by the King to form, not another Whig ministry, but a conservative coalition. Melbourne, however,

[1] N. Gash, 'F. R. Bonham: Conservative "Political Secretary", 1832–47', *E.H.R.*, lxiii, 502–22.

[2] N. Gash, *Reaction and Reconstruction* pp. 3–29 deals with the position of the Crown in the post-Reform Bill political situation. This account follows his very clear treatment.

refused, and Peel and the Conservative leaders agreed that such a task was impossible because of party differences which prevented the men whom the King desired in office from serving together. William now decided to resort to the more extreme step of dismissing the Whig ministry; and the opportunity arose in November 1834 when Melbourne proposed that Lord John Russell should become leader of the Commons in place of Althorp, who had succeeded to his father's title in the Lords. Russell's reforming ideas, particularly in relation to the Irish Church, made his advancement unacceptable to William; and this was the occasion of the dismissal of the Whigs by the King in November 1834, and the summoning of the Conservatives under Peel to office. The step was an extreme one, and for William had most unhappy consequences. The lack of nomination boroughs made it impossible for Peel to meet parliament and explain his policy before dissolving and holding a General Election; he could not run the risk of facing the House with his ministers in the Commons seeking re-election. A dissolution and General Election accordingly took place; but although the Election, held in January 1835, witnessed Conservative gains, it did not give Peel enough party support in the new parliament for him to survive. The numerous defeats which in the end forced him to resign in April made it clear that party feeling was too strong for the old convention – that members should support the ministry of the King's choice – to have any relevance; and such feeling made William's further attempts to revert to a coalition fruitless. Melbourne and the Whigs returned to office with Russell as leader of the House; William had thus to accept back into office a ministry which he had dismissed, because only that ministry enjoyed majority support in the Commons. His action, indeed, had exposed the limitations on his powers. It is true that for the remaining two years of his life, William kept up his interest in politics; and, with his complaints and criticisms, made life rather unpleasant for Melbourne. But this was all he could do; he could not take any drastic measure such as he had taken in 1834.

When Victoria came to the throne in 1837, the parliamentary position of the Whigs had declined; the 1837 General Election caused by William IV's death saw further Conservative gains. In such a political situation, with parties more nearly balanced, the area for the influence of the Crown was rather greater; and Victoria, who was tutored by Melbourne after her accession, was, unlike William IV, strongly pro-Whig. There is little doubt that in the political situation of the late 1830s this helped the Whigs to remain in office rather longer than they might otherwise have done. There was, for example, the so-called Bedchamber Incident in 1839. In May of that year, Melbourne resigned because of the somewhat precarious position of the Whigs in the House of Commons; his ministry had a majority of five votes on its decision to suspend the constitution of Jamaica. Peel was sent for, and as a token of the young Queen's confidence in her new ministry, asked that the ladies holding higher posts in the Queen's household should resign, some of these ladies being related to the outgoing Whig ministers. But the Queen objected to the request, and her exaggeration of it led Melbourne and the retiring Whig ministers to offer their continuing support in office. The offer was accepted and the Whigs remained in power until 1841. It should, however, be noted that even on the Jamaica vote, the Whigs had still a majority in the House, if a small one; and this remained true till in May 1841, they were defeated on a fiscal motion and, in Jun 1841, a motion of no confidence was carried against them by one vote. The decision was then taken to dissolve, although Melbourne was hesitant about it since he was not sure that the Queen's ministers, in whom she clearly put her trust, would secure a majority in the subsequent General Election. His apprehension was well-founded, for the Conservatives under Peel secured a majority of about eighty; and this in spite of the use of the Queen's name in the election on behalf of the Whigs, and in spite of the use of money from the Privy Purse to help Whig candidates. Party feeling in favour of the Conservatives was too strong for 'the Queen's confidence' to have any effect; and Conservative party organisation also played an active role in the General Election of 1841. Once Peel had his party majority in the House, there was no room for the Queen's wishes; Melbourne had to resign and Peel had to come into office. Melbourne succinctly compared the situation with the Bedchamber Incident; 'Peel was in a very different position now, backed by a large majority, to when the other overture was made', he told the Queen. 'He had the power *now* to extort what he pleased.'

The decade after the Reform Bill thus proved very unfavourable for the adoption by the Crown of an active partisan role in politics; as has been seen, this is partly explained by the disfranchising clauses of the bill and partly by the development of party organisation and party attitudes, to which the Reform Act and its implications contributed. And, indeed, the end of the decade witnessed the withdrawal of the Crown from an actively partisan role; this was largely due to the influence of Albert, whom Victoria married in 1840. It was not that the Queen withdrew from politics altogether, or ceased to take an interest; rather, under Albert's influence, she recognised the limitations which existed on her power, and was, on the whole, prepared to work within them.

If the Crown emerged from the post-Reform Act period bearing marks of defeat and decline, the other non-representative element in the Constitution, the House of Lords, emerged in a seemingly stronger position.[1] The Lords, after all, had not been swamped with new creations in 1832; the threat had been enough. Thus if the Whigs in the 1830s enjoyed a party majority in the Commons, they did not enjoy this in the Lords. Further, the Lords retained their amending powers intact. In the course of the 1830s a great number of Whig bills were indeed severely amended by the Lords, and such activity provoked outspoken demands in radical and reforming circles for a reform of the House of Lords and a curtailment of its powers. But, in fact, the Lords weathered the storm and no reform of this kind came to pass. Yet there were certain limitations on the full exercise of the Lords' powers. A determined ministry with a majority in the Commons and support in the country could, in the last resort, impose its will on the Lords. If this had happened in 1831–32, it could happen again; although, in fact, once the Reform Bill had passed, neither Whig inclination nor public interest made it very likely to do so. A more effective restraining influence in the 1830s proved to be the acceptance by the Conservative party under Peel of moderate and measured reform,[2] and a growing sense among the peers that to reject a bill supported by the Conservatives in the Commons would be to harm party interests. Political considerations of this kind, therefore, could act as a deterrent to indulgence by the Lords in reckless and extreme behaviour.

If the events of the 1830s showed that the scope for independent action by Crown and Lords was limited, they also pointed to the importance of the representative element in the Constitution, the House of Commons. A ministry did not need the support of King or Lords to survive; but it could not survive without support in

[1] *Ibid.*, pp. 30–46.

[2] See below, Section (iii) of this chapter.

the Commons. It has, indeed, been said that the period between the first and second Reform Acts was the 'Golden Age of the House of Commons'; or, to put it another way, the 'heyday of the Independent Member'. For the Act finally destroyed the manipulative connection between King and Commons by disfranchising the nomination boroughs; and yet its enfranchising clauses did not create an electorate large enough to require the adoption of extensive party organisation, attachment to party programmes and loyalty to party discipline. A member returned by one or more of the private and personal influences which survived the Reform Act of 1832 did not owe his election to party organisation or party programmes; thus once in the House he could enjoy a considerable degree of independence and did not always have to toe a party line. A ministry, then, needed the support of the Commons; but deprived of the assets which royal favour could put at its disposal, and not yet in possession of the advantages provided by rigid party discipline, it was to some degree at the mercy of the House, or of the 'Independent Member'; the member once described as one 'who could not be depended on'.[1] All this has a certain truth; and yet the ways in which party did exist in the 1830s should not be overlooked. As has been seen, party organisation, party spirit and party loyalty were present; and in the context of the politics of the decade, party provided a fairly firm basis for both government and opposition, without reducing the House to a 'voting machine' and the members to 'lobby fodder'.

Parliamentary reform, then, passed in a manner which focussed attention on popular opinion and new forces in society; it brought into being a Parliament which at least took account of these forces, even if it by no means allowed them dominance. And its provisions, along with the issues which it raised, provided the setting for the constitutional and political developments of the decade.

(ii) *Reform of the Municipal Corporations; Church Reform*

The achievement of parliamentary reform in 1832 held the implication that other institutions in State and Church might well come under reforming attack; and two likely targets were the Municipal Corporations of England and Wales and the Church

---

[1] Quoted in J. P. Mackintosh, *The British Cabinet* (2nd edn., 1968), p. 78. See also *ibid.*, pp. 83–99, for consideration of this point.

of England. Abuses were notoriously prevalent in both. The Corporations were varied in composition, having grown up irregularly over centuries, according to the granting of charters of incorporation. Most technically consisted of a number of free-men, originally members of trade guilds or companies of the borough, a governing body, magistrates and various officers; but the term 'Corporation' had, in the course of time, come to be applied almost solely to the governing body, which was usually self-electing and self-perpetuating. The Corporations thus were administered by tiny cliques, with little or no relation to the great majority of the inhabitants of the borough; and yet over those inhabitants they might, and often did, levy tolls and taxes. They were, moreover, frequently in possession, as trustees, of charitable bequests and other patronage; and these tended to be used either for their own private enjoyment, or for the purpose of influencing voters at elections. And if the Corporations could be accused of inefficiency and being out of touch with social needs, the same criticisms were applicable to the Church of England. Pluralism, maladministration and inequitable distribution of Church funds: these and other matters might well come under the scrutiny of reformers. Further, the dissenters outside the Church of England were in a position in some ways analagous to that of the inhabitants of the boroughs who did not belong to the Corpora-tions: persons whose status had not been recognised; who had to pay rates for the upkeep of an institution to which they did not belong; and who were dependent on that institution for the provision of various religious offices, such as baptism, marriage and burial. It was not, therefore, at all unlikely that reform would be carried forward in these ways after 1832. It was indeed ano-malous that persons who might enjoy the parliamentary franchise after the Reform Act should be debarred from participation in the affairs of their own boroughs; and the dissenters, having been among those who achieved a certain political advancement by the Reform Act, might well demand similar recognition in the boroughs, and also release from continued subjection to the Church of England.

In the case of the Corporations, there was also another, more technical, reason why parliamentary reform clearly implied the introduction of a measure for Corporation reform. This lay in the fact that by the disfranchisement of certain boroughs and the introduction of the £10 household voter into the remainder, the

Act deprived the Corporations of much of the electoral influence which they had previously exercised. In these changed circumstances, some Corporations lost their patrons, who withdrew the sums which they had previously paid to assist the return of their candidates, and those bodies which had depended on these sums to meet expenses were left destitute, and were in clear need of reform. But not all Corporations were in this category; many were still in possession of funds and bequests, and even with an enlarged electorate, continued to use these for electoral purposes after 1832. This point was, indeed, taken as providing a clear argument for reform. 'The most active spring of election bribery and villainy everywhere is known to be the Corporation system,' claimed *The Times* in 1833. '. . . The fact is that Parliamentary Reform, if it were not to include corporation reform likewise, would have been literally a dead letter, except in so far as the county representation be concerned.'[1] Moreover, with the Whigs in office with a great reforming majority after 1832, the question had a fair prospect of attention. In February 1833, indeed, in the first session of the reformed parliament, Althorp stated that he felt that the government should take action quickly. A Select Committee of the Commons was, therefore, appointed to inquire into the state of the Corporations of England and Wales, and to suggest remedial measures.

The Committee, however, found its task too extensive for it to complete, and recommended the appointment of a Royal Commission to carry out the investigation. This was implemented in July 1833; the twenty Commissioners appointed were mostly in the legal profession, with Joseph Parkes, a lawyer with great experience of electoral cases, as secretary, and John Blackburne, M.P. for Huddersfield, as chairman. The country was divided into districts, and the Commissioners were sent out, mostly in pairs, to investigate each and to send in reports on the Corporations which they found in existence. In October 1834, some sixteen months after the Commission had been appointed, the work was begun of arranging and ordering the material which had been collected, and throughout the winter of 1834–35, Parkes and Blackburne were occupied with the task of drafting a report. The first draft of this was circulated among the members of the Commission in February 1835; and less than a month later, after further consultations with the Commissioners, the report, in its final form, was presented to the Home Secretary.

[1] *The Times*, 25 June 1833.

The Commissioners had visited 285 towns and found 246 Corporations; and of these, the report made very strong criticisms. 'Even where,' it said, 'these institutions exist in their least imperfect form and are most rightfully administered, they are inadequate to the present state of society. In their actual condition, where not productive of positive evil, they exist in the great majority of instances, for no purpose of general utility. . . .' The report did not, in fact, recommend specific remedies, but expressed the view that a 'thorough reform' was necessary before the Corporations could become 'useful and efficient instruments of local government'.

The Commission, therefore, carried out its work quickly, and produced a cogent and lucid, if critical report. It was, indeed, strongly attacked on the grounds that it did its work too quickly, was too anxious to find material which told against the Corporations, and was unfair in its comments on them in the report. All these criticisms had a measure of truth. Parkes was determined to complete the investigations quickly so that legislation would not be long delayed; the majority of the Commissioners, with their radical sympathies, did not approach their task in an impartial state of mind; and their report made too sweeping a condemnation of the Corporations.[1] But as Parkes had hoped, it did prepare the ground for reform. He himself, indeed, had a share in drafting the bill for Corporation reform which was introduced by Lord John Russell in June 1835. The bill provided that one uniform system should replace all existing forms of government in 183 boroughs. This was to consist of a town council elected by all inhabitant householders of the borough of three years' standing. The existing freemen in the boroughs were to retain all their pecuniary and personal rights, including that of voting at parliamentary elections, for the rest of their lives, but the freeman qualification was not to be preserved beyond this. The council itself was to consist of one body only, elected for three years, a third retiring annually; and there was to be no property qualification for its members.

Unlike the Reform Bill, the Municipal Corporations Bill had a relatively smooth passage through the Commons. The reason was that its reforming principle was accepted by Peel[2] and the bulk of

[1] These points are developed in my article 'The Municipal Corporation Commission and Report, 1833–35' in *B.I.H.R.*, xxxvi, 36–52.

[2] Hansard, *Parl. Debates* 3rd ser., xxviii, 559, 831. See also below, Section (iii) of this chapter.

the Conservative party in the House. It is true that Peel did not like all the details of the bill. He was, for example, critical of the lack of any property qualification for town councillors and introduced an amendment – an unsuccessful one – which would have required such a qualification. But he did not offer any serious resistance to the bill as a whole, and it passed the Commons in July 1835, with its major provisions unscathed. But like the Reform Bill, the Corporation Bill ran into formidable opposition in the Lords, where its reforming principle was emphatically not accepted. To many of their Lordships, the Corporations were bulwarks of the old order and reassuring symbols of its survival against the onslaught of reform.[1] To those who saw the Corporations in this light, the rights and wrongs of their reform were beside the point; the mere fact that it was proposed at all was enough to provoke their implacable resistance. It was, they said, simply a party manoeuvre, designed to benefit the reformers and, moreover, the reform would be politically disastrous: Lyndhurst, who assumed a leading role in the Lords' opposition, warned their Lordships that if the Corporations fell 'the Church would come next and the hereditary peerage afterwards'.

The Lords, then, having been coerced into accepting the reform of parliament in 1832, felt that the time had come to make a stand. Feeling ran so high that the bill was allowed a second reading only on condition that counsel was heard at the bar on behalf of the boroughs which had presented petitions against it, and after this was concluded, lengthy evidence was taken in support of the allegations of such petitions. There was, indeed, talk of total rejection of the bill. Their Lordships were thus proving that there was fight left in them and that the Upper Chamber could prove a real obstacle. And yet the fact remained that the principle of the bill had secured the support of the Conservatives in the Commons; and to reject it would involve a split in the Conservative party. However unwelcome these considerations might be, they persuaded a sufficient number of ultras in the Lords not to take 'the leap of total rejection', as it was put; here then, was an instance of political considerations restraining extreme use of the Lords' constitutional powers. Yet this did not mean that the Lords did nothing; their policy was to go into Committee and there to amend the bill so completely that its reforming principle

[1] For elaboration of these points, see my article, 'The Politics of Municipal Reform, 1835,' in *E.H.R.*, LXXXI, 673–92.

was smothered. This, wrote Londonderry to Buckingham, would make the measure a 'Conservative arrangement'.[1] It was in this spirit that various 'wrecking amendments' were proposed. There were amendments to preserve the property and parliamentary status of freemen, and to require a property qualification for town councillors; to divide towns of more than six thousand inhabitants into wards; and perhaps most revealing of all, an amendment that one quarter of the town councillors elected under the new arrangements should hold office for life with the title of aldermen. All these arrangements were designed to safeguard privilege, property and the nominative, as opposed to the elective, principle in the government of the boroughs; and all were passed by massive majorities. Even this more restrained and subtle use of the Lord's power had, then, considerably reduced the reforming principle of the bill, and when it returned in amended form to the Commons on 28 August 1835 the possibility of a constitutional clash was still a real one.

In fact, however, the political situation induced a compromise. For one thing, the Whig government displayed a willingness to accept certain of the Lords' amendments: in particular those relating to the freemen, a property qualification for town councillors – and after much wrangling – the division into wards at six thousand inhabitants. It may be doubted if the government wanted to fight to the bitter end to save the entire bill; and even if it had so wanted, it was, perhaps, scarcely in a position to do so. William IV was in no mood to create peers to force the bill through the Lords. Further, unlike the crisis of 1831–2, there was little public interest in the reform, and this put the government in a weak position to bring pressure to bear on the King; and further, a dissolution and election on the issue of the bill might not have produced the desired result. Again, the lack of urgent popular interest relieved fear of public disorder should a compromise settlement with the Lords be reached. Yet more was involved in the settlement than the flexibility of the government, for on certain amendments, in particular that relating to life aldermen, it took a firmer line. Here, it was the attitude of Peel, and once again a restraining, if grudging, sense of party unity among the ultras in the Lords, which helped to resolve the matter. For Peel

---

[1] Duke of Buckingham and Chandos, *Memoirs of the Courts and Cabinets of William IV and Victoria* (1861), ii, 198. See also G. Kitson Clark, *Peel and the Conservative Party, A Study in Party Politics, 1832–41* (2nd edn., 1964), pp. 277–8.

did not consider the amendment introducing life aldermen an improvement on the bill, and supported the government in its refusal to accept it. This meant that the ultras in the Lords could persevere in it only at the cost of splitting the party, a cost which, in the end, they proved unwilling to pay. Yet even here, a measure of flexibility on the part of the government smoothed the path, for a class of aldermen, elected by the councillors and serving for six years was to be introduced into the reformed boroughs. Thus the Whigs had lacked the inclination to press the original proposals of the bill too far, and, in the absence of popular pressure, saw no necessity to do so; the ultras deserted by Peel, were restrained from extreme behaviour. The matter was, then, settled by a process of political compromise and negotiation, and the bill finally passed in September 1835.

The Municipal Corporations Act applied to 178 boroughs in England and Wales; five boroughs were removed from the original number in the bill. It established an uniform municipal electorate of all male inhabitant ratepayers of three years' standing;[1] and a town council composed of councillors, who were directly elected, and aldermen and mayor, who were indirectly elected. The councillors served for a period of three years, one third retiring annually and being eligible for re-election. The councillors as a body elected one third of their number to be aldermen either from their own ranks or from men qualified to be councillors; the aldermen served for six years, one half retiring, and being eligible for re-election after three years. The councillors and aldermen together annually elected a mayor from their own ranks. Boroughs not affected by the Act – and they included boroughs such as Manchester which had not been incorporated and were thus beyond the scope of the reform – could apply for incorporation under the terms of the Act; and although this was costly and, on occasion, caused local controversy, the process went on steadily thereafter.

It will be seen that the municipal franchise made no mention of a £10 house. It is true that there was the residence and rate-paying requirement; yet the lack of a property qualification made the municipal electorate more democratic than the parliamentary. It appears, however, that this point should not be exaggerated. Calculations made by Keith-Lucas, in 39 boroughs where the

---

[1] In fact, this proved to be two years and eight months, since residence was taken as up to the end of August in any year and the whole of the two previous years.

two electorates may be fairly compared, show that in 1837, the municipal qualification enfranchised only an additional 20–25 per cent. It seems clear, then, that the majority of houses valued at less than £10 a year were excluded from the municipal electorate; and from the various reasons which might be advanced for this, Keith-Lucas concludes that the houses of the working classes were not rated at all, and thus their occupants would not be eligible to enjoy the municipal franchise.[1] The effects of the Act in this respect, therefore, appear to have been rather less democratic than might be thought. Further, the qualifications required of councillors ensured that property had a powerful voice on the town council. An analysis of the first town council elected under the terms of the Act at Leicester shows it to be composed almost entirely of local tradesmen, shopkeepers and bankers, with a certain sprinkling of 'professional' men, such as doctors.[2] The activities of many newly elected town councils after 1835 were, indeed, characteristic of property-owners, for the councils were much concerned with measures which provided for the proper management of corporate property and the maintenance of public order. Attention was given to the task of putting borough finances in order, usually by a policy of economy and retrenchment; and the other preoccupation of the new councils in their early years was the establishment and ordering of a police force, which was, in fact, incumbent on them under the terms of the Act. After the extravagance and disorderliness of the old Corporations, it is understandable that such a programme should have first priority; but it was one which was scarcely compatible with the provision of social amenities for the boroughs. The task of social improvement was not, in fact, always vested in the town councils. Under the unreformed system, such responsibilities as paving and cleansing had often been looked after by Improvement Commissioners, elected by ratepayers, and although the Municipal Corporations Act gave the opportunity for such responsibilities to be transferred to the new town councils, this could only happen on the option of the Commissioners. In fact, it happened only very gradually. In terms of representation and function, then, the effects of the Act embraced only a limited

[1] B. Keith-Lucas, *The English Local Government Franchise. A Short History* (Oxford, 1952), pp. 63, 67.

[2] A. Temple Patterson, *Radical Leicester* (Leicester, 1954), p. 215 fn 1. See also H. J. Dyos (ed.), *The Study of Urban History* (1968), p. 315 ff.

section of the local community; it was still 'men of property' and not simply 'men' who were represented and catered for.

Nevertheless, the Act did firmly establish the electoral principle in local borough government; and although modifications have been made and further changes may not be long delayed,[1] the basic structure of the town council which it created has remained essentially the same to this day. And if the Act was of most benefit to the property owners of the borough, they were, at least, the 'new' property owners, who at this level of borough government made far greater strides than they had yet done in parliament; the Municipal Corporations Act represented a much more immediate and substantial gain for the urban middle classes than the Reform Act had done. Further, although the Act did not create anything approaching the modern all-purpose local authority, it did create in the town council the agency which, in time, was to undertake and be charged with more and more functions designed to improve the condition of the town and the general environment of its inhabitants.

If Corporation reform thus followed within three years of Parliamentary reform, the Church of England was likewise soon subjected to attention and adaptation. The Whigs, indeed, had plans early in the decade for something approaching a Reform Bill for the Church; these included the creation of new sees to take account of population changes and a re-distribution of the wealth of the Church by reducing the income of the richest bishoprics and giving the surplus to poorer parishes. However, little was achieved at this stage; and the matter was taken up again by Peel while he was in office in 1834–35. Although very much concerned to uphold the Church as an established institution, Peel was ready to sponsor internal reforming measures. A Commission was, therefore, appointed to inquire into various aspects of the state of the Church in England and Wales, and its first report in 1835 suggested much the same reforms as those proposed by the Whigs: the creation, for example, of new sees at Ripon and Manchester and the re-distribution of church income. But so short-lived was Peel's Ministry that it fell to the Whigs to implement reform proposals. Thus the Established Church Act of 1836 went some way in the direction of standardising the territorial responsibilities of bishoprics and re-apportioning

[1] In view of the Royal Commission at present (1969) investigating the matter.

church income; and more important, it set up a permanent body, the Ecclesiastical Commission, which was to administer these changes and to recommend further reforms. With the establishment of this body, which contained dignitaries of Church and of State, and to which all bishops belonged after 1840, the Church gained an agency designed to frame 'Church measures' for parliament and to put them into effect once passed; a body which would thus reform the Church from within. In this it achieved a fair measure of success, and, before the end of the thirties, many of the abuses which had attracted attention at the beginning of the decade – such as maldistribution of sees, gross inequalities in episcopal incomes and pluralism – had, in fact, been removed, and the Church was able to hold its head higher.

The redress of dissenters' grievances also received attention from both parties in the thirties, although here the Whigs were more willing to make concessions than the Tories, and the chronological sequence of this process was rather similar to that of Church reform. Once again, the matter was raised early in the decade. In May 1833, a United Committee of Dissenters issued a number of grievances on which relief was sought;[1] and these included the payment of Church rates, the fact that the Anglican marriage ceremony was compulsory, the absence of any legal registration of births and deaths – the only record being with the Church of England – and the exclusion of dissenters from the ancient English universities. In 1834 the Whigs attempted to meet some of these points with a Church Rates bill and a measure granting some relief from the marriage laws; but these were not satisfactory to all dissenters – who were by no means completely united in their wants – and were abandoned. Peel also tried to remedy certain of the dissenters' grievances; a Dissenters' Marriage bill was introduced in the course of his ministry, but again without success. In 1836, however, the Whigs finally granted the dissenters some satisfaction. A civil register of births, marriages and deaths was introduced, thereby breaking the Church of England's monopoly in the recording of such matters; and it became lawful for marriages to be held in places of worship other than an Anglican church, provided that it was properly licensed for the purpose and the civil registrar was present.[2] Also in 1836, a

---

[1] N. Gash, *Reaction and Reconstruction*, p. 66.

[2] E. Halévy, *A History of the English People in the Nineteenth Century* (first published in English, 1927), iii, 201.

measure introduced by Russell provided for the commutation of tithes to a money payment; and between 1836 and 1838 formal and permanent recognition was given to the non-sectarian college which had been set up in London in 1828; as a teaching body, to be known as University College, it became part of the University of London, which was now newly incorporated as a degree giving body. But the question of admission to the ancient Universities was not achieved; and the dissenters were also denied satisfaction on the question of Church rates. In 1837, a Church Rates bill was, indeed, introduced, which would have had the effect of making the Church itself financially responsible for the upkeep of its fabric; but it ran into trouble, even among the Whigs,[1] and came to nothing. Thus, if some measure of redress was accorded to the dissenters, this was by no means as much as had been hoped for on their part.

The Reform Act of 1832 did, then, prove to be the prelude to further reforms in State and Church. Corporation reform, Church reform, relief of dissenters' grievances; all were part of a process of adapting and liberalising institutions and advancing the cause of hitherto subjected sections of the community. What was accomplished should not, of course, be exaggerated, and was a disappointment to many; but it was, nevertheless, a solid and substantial achievement.

(iii) *Reform and Reformers in Decline*

It has been seen that the passing of the Reform Act in 1832 had posed the question of how far reform should proceed: whether the Act was its terminal or its starting point. And, as was mentioned at the beginning of this study, the political reaction to this question marked the broad party divisions of the decade: Radical, Whig and Tory. The Municipal Corporations Act in 1835 raised very much the same point. To the Radicals, it was a welcome sign that reform was proceeding, not as fast as they would have liked, but at a reasonable rate; and that there was promise of more to come.[2] The Whigs, however, were much more cautious than this. Russell simply described the Municipal Corporations Bill as 'in strict accordance with the spirit and intention of the Reform Act . . . a measure to reform one of our most valuable institutions, and at

[1] N. Gash, *Reaction and Reconstruction*, pp. 72–3.

[2] See below, Chapter 3 (i).

the same time to preserve it . . .'. The Whigs, moreover, did not share the radical vision of reform moving forward with ever-increasing momentum. It is true that certain Whigs were more willing than others to take reform further, but none ever had an appetite for 'scything reform'. Even Russell, who, on occasion – as in 1834 over the question of appropriating Irish church funds to secular purposes – had gone beyond the limits thought desirable by many of his colleagues, refused to countenance any measures for further parliamentary reform, such as the ballot, shorter parliaments or an extension of the suffrage. In 1837, he earned the nickname of 'Finality Jack' by his statement that the Act of 1832 was a 'final measure'. Further, if the Whigs showed little in-clination to fulfil the hopes of the radicals, the post-Reform Act propertied electorate was to show even less. A great reforming majority had, indeed, been returned by the General Election of December 1832; but already by 1835, this majority was consider-ably reduced by the Election of that year, and it was reduced even further by the Election of 1837. In circumstances of increasing parliamentary difficulties at the end of the decade, the Whigs did make one concession in the direction of further reform by making the ballot an open question in 1839; but this was an attempt rather to recoup their declining fortunes than a manifes-tation of genuine reforming zeal. It was, however, an attempt which was out of place in a political nation increasingly dominated by a desire for consolidation in the affairs of State and Church, and not change; and, indeed, out of tune with the social and economic problems which beset the country in the throes of an economic depression which set in at the end of the decade. If in 1841 the Whigs tried to come to terms with these new problems by advocating a measure of free trade, the attempt came too late to redeem their position.

The years after 1835, then, witnessed the growing disillusion-ment of the radicals; the disinclination and steady decline of the 'reformers'; and the gradual rise of the 'resisters' to political pre-eminence. But from the mid-decade, the distinction between the party of reform and the party of resistance was not completely clear-cut. For, as has been seen, Peel and the bulk of the Tory party in the Commons were prepared to accept the principle of reform as manifested in the Municipal Corporations Bill in 1835; and this was an indication of the change which had come about in the Tory party since the struggles over parliamentary reform in 1831–32. The virtual annihilation of the Tories in the first election under the reformed system, in December 1832, had shown that mere resistance to change had no political future; the Reform Act must be accepted as a political fact, and Toryism must accommodate itself to the post-Reform Act world. It must still be the party of defence;[1] there was, indeed, in the view of Peel, great need for such a party at a time when reform threatened to invade and make serious inroads on established institutions. But 'defence' could not mean simply putting up the barriers against all reform; this would spell political disaster and merely provide targets for radical attack. Rather, the party must at least acquiesce in moderate and measured reform in the institutions of State and Church, which would remove their worst defects and thereby save them from radical reform at the hands of their enemies. Thus in the Tamworth Manifesto, issued at the time of the General Election of 1835, Peel acknowledged that the Reform Act was a 'final and irrevocable settlement of a great constitutional question; a settlement which no friend to the peace and welfare of (the) country would attempt to disturb'. As to the spirit of the Act, he would not accept it if it meant that 'we are to live in a perpetual vortex of agitation'; there would, then, be resistance to radical aspirations. But if that spirit implied merely a 'careful review of institutions, civil and ecclesiastical, undertaken in a friendly temper, combining with the firm maintenance of established rights the correction of proved abuses and the redress of real grievances', then Peel undertook to act 'in such a spirit and with such intentions'.[2]

Toryism thus shaded into Conservatism; and the Conservative party became more sophisticated than the party of pure resistance. It was in accordance with the Tamworth Manifesto that Peel did not interrupt the progress of the Municipal Corporations Commission during his short-lived ministry of 1834–35, and that he sponsored Church reform and dissenter relief. It was in this spirit that once out of office and on the return of the Whigs in April 1835, he supported the principle of the Municipal Corporation Bill, even if the Bill might, in his view, require amendment to make it more 'conservative' of the interests of property and stability. On Church matters, he was, it is true, unwilling to

---

[1] N. Gash, *Reaction and Reconstruction*, p. 148.
[2] See extracts from the Tamworth Manifesto reprinted in G. M. Young and W. D. Handcock (eds.), *English Historical Documents XII (1), 1833–1874* (1956), 127–131. (Hereafter cited as 'Young and Handcock'.)

support certain proposals of the Whigs, such as the admission of
Dissenters to the ancient Universities, but he gave the Whigs his
backing on internal Church reform. His policy was seldom free of
criticism. It was disliked by the radicals, who felt that it was blur-
ring the line of demarcation between the parties and holding up
the progress of real reform. It was disliked, too, by the ultras in
Peel's own party, who wanted the party to remain one of pure
resistance to reform. But despite such criticisms, Peel persisted in
his policy; after 1835 he supported the Whigs in the 'conservative'
interest, and was in no hurry to dispossess them of office until his
party had a strong position in the Commons, which would be a
secure basis for a Conservative government.

The fact that it was able to achieve this in 1841, within ten
years of the virtual annihilation of the Tories in 1832, was
remarkable. It was to some extent due to the shortcomings of its
opponents. There was, indeed, little difference between Whigs
and Conservatives on a number of issues; but the Whigs always
gave the impression of being susceptible to radical pressures. After
the Election of 1835, indeed, their parliamentary position
depended on radical and Irish support, and they became the
unwilling prisoners of their own past professions of sympathy for
reform. But on the positive side, the Conservative revival was due
to efficient party organisation, which exploited the rather for-
tuitous circumstance of three Elections occurring in such rapid
succession in 1835, 1837 and 1841 all three, moreover, engendering party spirit; and, of course, to the leadership and policy of
Peel, with its assurance of government which would be strong,
orderly and anti-radical, but not reactionary. It was an assurance
which contrasted very favourably with the impression given by the
Whigs of drift and indecision, and one which seemed to have
particular merits at a time when the economic crisis of the late
thirties was engendering social discontent and the threat of disorder. That it was an assurance which clearly accorded with the
desire of the political nation was fully and finally seen in the
General Election of 1841 and the large parliamentary majority
which the Conservatives enjoyed as a result of it. With Peel and
the Conservatives in office, the institutions of State and Church
were, indeed, safe from radical reform; but by a twist of political
fortune, the party built around such constitutional and religious
questions was forced to face the economic and social problems
prevalent at the time of its arrival in power. (See below, Chapter 4.)

CHAPTER TWO

Reform: Government and Society

(i) Factory Reform

Legislation regulating hours and conditions in factories first reached the statute book in 1802, and thereafter, largely as a result of the interest and initiative of individual Members of Parliament, further proposals on the subject were put before and passed the unreformed House.[1] The 1830s did not, therefore, mark an entirely new departure in this direction, but in the early years of the decade, the matter assumed greater prominence and certain important developments took place. In Yorkshire, a popular movement came into being to press for a shorter working day. Drawing its support from certain evangelical Tories, acting from paternal and charitable concern, and from factory workers organised in short-time committees, this Ten Hour Movement kept up a steady and well ordered campaign to achieve its aim of a ten-hour day. Factory reform also evoked considerable interest and activity in parliamentary and 'official' circles. After the passage of a further Act in 1831, the whole question of factory hours and conditions underwent extensive examination and inquiry by a parliamentary Select Committee and a Royal Commission; and there followed in 1833 another Act, which had various novel and important features.

The Act of 1831 was much in accordance with earlier legislation, and owed its origin to Sir John Cam Hobhouse, who had been associated with a previous measure in the 1820s. Hobhouse's proposals in 1831 were to limit the hours worked by children and young persons in textile factories. They prohibited all employment under the age of nine and all night work between nine and eighteen; and for those between these two ages, the working day was to be limited to eleven and a half hours. The limitations envisaged by the bill were not, in fact, very much more stringent than those imposed by earlier acts, but they met with strong resistance from manufacturers and millowners. The restrictions and regulations, they argued, would mean a reduction in output, loss

[1] M. W. Thomas, *The Early Factory Legislation* (1948), pp. 9–13, 17–29.

of markets, a lowering of wages: economic setback, in short, for masters and men alike. Thus, under strong pressure, Hobhouse had to accept several amendments to his bill, and the Act, which passed in October 1831, was even less stringent than the original proposals. It applied only to cotton factories; nine remained the age below which work was prohibited, but the proposals regulating night work were weakened by a shortening of the hours defined as such, and the working day for children and young persons between nine and eighteen was extended to twelve hours. Further, in common with previous legislation, no machinery was established to ensure the effective enforcement of such limitations as the Act did impose.[1]

Although Hobhouse's Act made relatively little contribution to the development of factory legislation, the episode was not without effect on the popular factory movement already in existence. Active in the cause was Richard Oastler, steward of a large estate at Fixby, near Huddersfield; a strong Anglican, Oastler laid great stress on good works and charitable causes, and his Toryism was highly paternalistic in character. His career as a factory reformer began in 1830, when, on a visit to a factory owner in Bradford, John Wood, who entertained severe misgivings about factory conditions, Oastler was overcome with shame that such matters had never previously troubled him; and he gave a promise to Wood that he would attempt to improve the position.[2] Immediately on his return to Fixby, Oastler composed a letter entitled 'Yorkshire Slavery' – the first of what was to be a series under that title – and sent it to the *Leeds Mercury*.[3] The letter made great play with the fact that several prominent local manufacturers were enthusiastic supporters of the anti-slavery movement; and its argument was to the effect that they need not go to the West Indies to discover slavery, but could find it in their own factories. To Oastler, Hobhouse's proposals were a step in the right direction, and he was prepared to accept an eleven and a half hour day between the ages of nine and eighteen. This was, moreover, true of those factory workers and working class sympathisers who, from the late 1820s, had been campaigning for reform; in

[1] *Ibid.*, pp. 29–31.

[2] C. Driver, *Tory Radical, The Life of Richard Oastler* (New York, 1946), pp. 39–42.

[3] Reprinted *ibid.*, pp. 42–44.

Yorkshire, short-time committees were, indeed, widely established to agitate for the adoption of Hobhouse's bill. But when the bill encountered opposition and obstruction from the manufacturers, Oastler grew more militant and came out in favour of a ten-hour day; and there also developed much closer co-operation between Oastler and the factory workers. Since Hobhouse had succumbed to pressure to weaken the terms of his bill, both realised that a new spokesman had to be found; and the pressure in itself provided clear evidence that a concerted campaign was necessary to over-come opposition. Thus, although on political and religious grounds, there was a wide gulf between the predominantly dis-senting and radical short-time committees and the Tory and Anglican Oastler, both saw the urgency to make common cause in the Ten Hour Movement.

It was, then, this movement which made all the running for further reform. In late 1831, a new parliamentary champion was found in Michael Sadler, a close friend of Oastler. Sadler came from a Leeds family of linen merchants, and after a period as a linen importer, he embarked on a parliamentary career as a Tory. Like Oastler, Sadler was a strong Churchman of evangelical out-look and social conscience, much concerned with good works; and he was, therefore, sympathetic to an approach made by Oastler and three prominent short-time committees requesting that he should sponsor a factory bill to accord with the views of the Ten Hour Movement. He was given leave to do this in December 1831, and in March 1832 introduced a bill which proposed that no child should enter a factory below the age of nine; that all between nine and eighteen should have a ten-hour day, exclusive of meal times, and that there should be no night work under the age of twenty-one. In his speech introducing the bill, Sadler strongly brought out the philanthropic and paternalistic approach to the question, so characteristic of his and Oastler's attitude – that some-thing had to be done to remedy the conditions in which human beings were being forced to work.[1] His efforts, moreover, received strong backing at the 'popular' level; Oastler and his collaborators in the Ten Hour Movement realised the need for arousing and sustaining interest and support by propaganda and organisation. Broadsheets, pamphlets and tracts were issued, arguing the case

[1] Extract printed in E. Royston Pike, *Human Documents of the Industrial Revolution in Britain* (1966), pp. 117–20.

for reform; short-time committees were set up in small villages as
in large towns, and a central short-time committee was set up in
Leeds to co-ordinate and supervise their activities. The factory
movement, moreover, spread outside Yorkshire; in Lancashire
attention hitherto directed mainly towards trade union activities
now embraced factory regulation as well, and short-time committees were set up, with a central committee in Manchester.

Yet in spite of all this effort and activity, there remained formidable difficulties and obstacles. Sadler was given leave to bring
his bill to a second reading only on condition that it was referred
to a Select Committee of the House of Commons; much disappointed, he had to accept this condition, although he himself
was to be chairman of the Committee. The Ten Hour Movement
was highly indignant at what it regarded as the shelving of the
matter in this way; just as Hobhouse's bill had been defeated by
intrigue, so Sadler's was being thwarted by a procedural device.
A vast amount of energy and organisation went into plans to meet
the Select Committee; the central committee at Leeds planned
and classified the kind of information which would be sought by
members of the Committee, and this scheme was then transmitted
to each of the short-time committees. Their work was to assemble
the local evidence, sift and verify it and then forward it to the
central committee for comparison and co-ordination with the
returns from other districts. A great deal of emphasis was placed
on the necessity for committees and witnesses to speak only on
matters of which they had personal experience, and in this way,
all witnesses who were finally chosen to go before the Select
Committee in London had their credentials carefully tested.[1]

Despite all this effort, however, further disappointments were
ahead. With the question of parliamentary reform still dominating
the political situation, parliament was prorogued and dissolved in
December 1832. The General Election of that month, it is true,
gave the movement an opportunity to publicise its case, but one
result in the Election represented a severe setback. This was at
Leeds, where Sadler had accepted an invitation from local
Tories to contest the borough, granted parliamentary representation for the first time by the Reform Act. The Leeds election of
December 1832 thus attracted considerable attention to the fac-

---

[1] The 'Confidential Memorandum' which was used by the short-time
committees in preparation of their evidence for the Select Committee is reprinted in C. Driver, *op. cit.*, pp. 550–53.

tory question; but it was a great blow to the Ten Hour Movement when Sadler was defeated. At this point, then, December 1832 to January 1833, the outlook was bleak. The movement had to find a new parliamentary spokesman, and lobbying had to be carried out at Westminster. Oastler himself felt that the Reform Act had hindered rather than helped the cause; in his view, the Act had simply entrenched the capitalists and manufacturers, the opponents of the Ten Hour Movement, in power. And at the popular level, there was the need to keep up morale by further agitation and organisation.

In January 1833, however, the movement received a fillip with the publication of the report of the Select Committee. The Committee had sat on forty-three days between April and August 1832. Sadler, the chairman, was not, of course, unprejudiced, but the Committee included a number of known opponents of the Ten Hour Movement. Nevertheless, the report made stark revelations about factory hours and conditions; moreover, it received wide publicity, and brought the whole question to the notice of many who had previously been unaware of it. Again, the movement acquired a new parliamentary spokesman in Lord Ashley, son and heir of the sixth Earl of Shaftesbury, and Tory member for Dorset. He was approached by Rev. George Stringer Bull, a prominent member of the Ten Hour Movement, and agreed to act on its behalf; and here again, it appears that his motives were inspired by charitable and humanitarian considerations – his decision was taken after 'meditation and prayer.'[1] Thus when the new session opened, on 5 February 1833, Ashley announced that he would re-introduce Sadler's bill. Once more, the Ten Hour Movement rose in support; meetings and demonstrations were held in Yorkshire and Lancashire on a scale greater than ever before. Many of these were addressed by Oastler himself; his speeches struck a new note of urgency and stressed the need for quick action if social disorder was to be avoided.

But a further setback to the popular movement was to come. On the same day that Ashley introduced the Ten Hour Bill – 5 March 1833 – one of the most able spokesmen for the manufacturers in the House of Commons, Wilson Patten, Tory member for North Lancashire, proposed that there should be a further inquiry, this time by a Royal Commission. He claimed that the Sadler Committee had heard only the operatives' point of view;

[1] C. Driver, *op. cit.*, pp. 212–13.

the adjournment of Parliament had prevented the manufacturers from putting their case, and had they been able to do so, their evidence would have redressed the balance. Patten's motion was not actually debated until 3 April, but it was carried by one vote – seventy-four to seventy-three. A Royal Commission was, therefore, set up on 19 April to investigate the employment of children in factories. From this point, then, the question was to be dealt with at the 'official' level; it was virtually removed from the hands of the Ten Hour Movement, which, having taken so much of the initiative, was now reduced to a role of protest and recrimination.[1]

The new arrangement did not, however, mean that the question was lost sight of or action unduly postponed or delayed. The commission set an extremely fast pace in its proceedings and completed its work remarkably quickly; indeed, the first draft of the report was in the hands of the government within forty-five days, and it was duly presented and published in June 1833. Moreover, any suspicions that the commission would 'whitewash' the manufacturers proved to be false. The report did not attempt to conceal evidence of long hours worked in bad conditions, and, more especially, of the harmful effects which these had on children in factories; and it made specific recommendations for remedy and reform.[2]

Nevertheless, there were differences between the 'official' and the 'unofficial' approaches to the question. Whereas the attitude of the Ten Hour Movement had been much influenced by charitable and humanitarian concern, the Royal Commission looked at the matter in a rather more dispassionate light. The commissioners were men ruled by the head rather than by the heart; in their view, bad social conditions were to be condemned not so much because of human suffering and degradation which they caused, but more on the grounds that they brought about a great wastage in human resources and betrayed a sad lack of administrative efficiency. This wastage and inefficiency, they considered, could be avoided and put to rights by planning and forethought. Such an approach was much in accordance with Benthamite ideas; and, indeed, several members of the commission, including its secretary, John Wilson and two of the London central board, Edwin Chadwick and Southwood Smith, had been friends of

[1] See below, Chapter 3 (i).

[2] Extracts are given in Young and Handcock, pp. 934–49.

Jeremy Bentham. The commissioners were, then, 'disinterested men, cool, analytical and unsentimental . . . model social scientists'.[1] And this was reflected in their Report. Such matters as the structure of factories, arrangements for drainage and ventilation, and the provision of facilities for washing were singled out for attention; and they were considered to have an important bearing on the health and well-being of the workpeople. Factories in which these matters were well arranged were held up as models of what could be achieved by careful planning and attention to detail; thus Deanston in Perthshire was commended on this account and the workpeople there said to be 'cheerful' and 'happy-looking'. Good environment, then, led to health and happiness; a contented, and, by implication, an efficient labour-force. Again, the report was rather less preoccupied than the Ten Hour Movement and its spokesmen with the alleged cruelties practised on children, since it held that they were not inherent in the factory system; it was concerned rather with the long hours worked by children which *were* inherent in the system. And the effects of these long hours were spelled out in rather clinical terms: 'permanent deterioration of the physical constitution: the production of disease often wholly irremediable and the partial and entire exclusion (by reason of excessive fatigue) from the means of obtaining adequate education and acquiring useful habits, or of profiting by these means when afforded'. Emphasis was, then, laid less on human suffering than on waste of human resources: the commissioners were primarily concerned with the impairment of the body and the lack of training for the mind.

Again, whereas the Ten Hour Movement envisaged the regulation of adults' hours of work, the commissioners were prepared to recommend only the regulation of hours worked by children. In the words of the report: 'at the age when children suffer . . . injuries from the labour they undergo, they are not free agents, but are let out to hire, the wages they earn being received and appropriated by their parents or guardians. We are therefore of opinion that a case is made out for the interference of the legislature on behalf of the children employed in factories.' Any more comprehensive measure of protection was ruled out, both on principle, since it involved interference with hours of 'free agents'; and because it would lead to what the report called 'very serious practical evils' – presumably the evils usually felt

[1] J. T. Ward, *The Factory Movement, 1830–1855* (1962), p. 94.

likely to follow restriction of adult hours – loss of production, trade, markets. Thus the Ten Hours Bill introduced by Ashley was severely criticised by the report because it would, in the view of the commissioners, lead to a ten hour day for adults; and the Ten Hour Movement was attacked by the report for – as it alleged – deliberately exploiting the plight of children in its propaganda to win popular support for a measure which would lead to a ten hour day for adults. And a further criticism made of Ashley's bill was that it made no provision 'for the occupation of any part of the time of children for their own benefit, either before or after their hours of labour', and took 'no charge of their education ilementary or moral'.

The 'official' solution to the problem was, then, rather different rrom the 'unofficial'. The commissioners recommended that there should be no employment in a factory for any child under nine; and this was in agreement with Ashley's bill. But thereafter, protection should extend only to the end of the thirteenth year: no child between nine and thirteen should work for more than eight hours a day and night work between 10 p.m. and 5 a.m. was to be prohibited. Thus in the view of the commissioners, the period of childhood ended with the close of the thirteenth year; after that, they claimed that the body was able to undertake longer hours of work, and the young person was free of parental control, able to make his or her own contract; and might be properly regarded as an adult and a 'free agent'. Further, to prevent any reduction of the hours worked by adults which the restriction under the age of thirteen might entail, the report recommended that a plan of working double sets of children be adopted; in other words, a shift system should be introduced so that adults might work their normal hours. And the report also recommended the provision of education for children in factories: 'since the whole of our recommendations have for their object the care and benefit of the children, we have been desirous of devising means for securing the occupation of a portion of the time abridged from their hours of labour to their own advantage. We think the best mode of accomplishing this object will be the occupation, suppose of three (or four) hours of every day in education . . .'.

The most notable departure by the commissioners from the earlier attempts at factory regulation, however, was over the question of the enforcement of legislation; and here the report had new and important recommendations to make. Sadler and Ashley had made little advance on the provisions introduced by Hobhouse's Act of 1831: that the parent was to provide a baptismal certificate which would give the age of the child, and that a time book should be kept in the factories so that there was a check on the hours worked. Ashley's bill proposed to increase the penalties for the evasion of such regulations: if a manufacturer wittingly accepted a false certificate of age, he was to be liable to a fine of £100, and the fine for making a false entry in the time book was to be increased to a maximum of £100.[1] But the Royal Commission report was highly critical of all such arrangements whereby the enforcement of the law was left to those who had an interest in breaking it. The parents of the child, with the prospect of being deprived of his wages, might well be tempted to alter the age on the certificate; and the manufacturers, faced with the possibility of losing cheap child labour and having the work schedule of their factories interrupted, had, in the words of the report, 'no especial motive to exert vigilance'. The report thus recommended that the enforcement of the law should be put into the hands of disinterested parties and that emphasis should be placed less on age, which could be easily forged, than on physical condition, which alone was the proper qualification for employment. A surgeon or doctor living in the town where the factory was situated should, therefore, examine any child entering the factory and give a certificate that the child was 'of the full growth and usual condition of a child of the age prescribed by the legislature (i.e. nine years of age) and fitted for employment in a manufactory'; and in case the doctor should be a friend of the parent, this certificate had to be given in the presence of a magistrate, who should countersign it. But of greater significance was the recommendation of the report that inspectors be appointed to ensure the effective operation of the legislation. This was based partly on the representations of certain manufacturers who wanted uniformity of practice, so that no one should get an unfair advantage by breaking the law; and it was reinforced by the consideration that little voluntary support was likely to be forthcoming for the application of a provision which applied only to children and was not conducive to the interests either of the manufacturers or of the adult workers. The report therefore recommended that three inspectors be appointed by the government to go round the chief

[1] M. W. Thomas, *op. cit.*, p. 44.

manufacturing districts, with powers to enter factories where children were employed, to ensure that the law was being observed, and to fine for neglect. The inspectors should, on occasion, meet as a board, report to the government on their proceedings, and suggest any amendments which they might consider necessary.

If there was the 'unofficial' and the 'official' approaches to the question of factory reform, it was the latter which prevailed. Ashley's bill had not, indeed, been withdrawn, and when it came up for its second reading on 17 June 1833, Althorp, on behalf of the government, said that he would not oppose it at that stage since the Royal Commission report would soon be available and the House would want to consider its suggestions. But once the report was presented on 25 June, it became clear that the Ten Hour Bill was acceptable neither to the government nor to the House; and Ashley surrendered his bill. Thus on 9 August, a bill prepared by Chadwick and bearing a close resemblance to the report, was introduced for the government by Althorp. It had a rapid passage through parliament, and on 29 August 1833, received the royal assent.

The Act applied to all textile factories, with the exception of the lace trade. There was to be no employment under the age of nine; children between nine and thirteen[1] were to work for not more than forty-eight hours in a week, or nine hours in any one day; and a further provision, which owed its origin not to the commissioners but to Althorp, limited the hours of young persons between thirteen and eighteen to not more than sixty-nine in a week, or twelve in any one day. There was to be no night work – defined as between 8.30 p.m. and 5.30 a.m. – under the age of eighteen. The Act also required children between nine and thirteen to attend a school. Again, the question of enforcement was faced, and the solution was much as the report recommended: no child between nine and thirteen could be employed in any factory without a certificate to the effect that he was 'of the ordinary strength and appearance' of a child of or exceeding nine; this certificate was to be given by a surgeon or doctor of the neigh-

[1] This provision was to be implemented gradually. After six months from the passing of the Act, no child under eleven was to be employed in a factory without a certificate to the effect that he was of the ordinary strength and appearance of a child of nine; after eighteen months, the age limit was to be raised to twelve, and after thirty months, thirteen.

bourhood, who had to examine the child, and the certificate had to be countersigned by a magistrate within three months. Further, four inspectors were to be appointed to ensure that the Act was put into effect and were given powers to this end.

Bearing in mind its 'official nature', it was to be expected that the Act should prove unpopular with the supporters of the Ten Hour Movement;[1] but it also received an unfavourable reception from many manufacturers, who regarded it as an unwarrantable intrusion into their private business arrangements. Although the Act did not apply to the hours worked by adults, it did threaten to affect these hours, for work done by adults in factories often depended on the performance of other duties by children; thus the reduction in children's hours and the time to be spent on education would affect the whole labour force. The solution to this, in the view of the framers of the Act, was the introduction of a relay system of child labour; and the spreading of the implementation of the Act over thirty months had been designed to give the owners time to organise such a system. But in many cases, it did not have this effect; the owners objected that relays were difficult to run efficiently and that they interrupted the routine of the factory. There was also a strong body of opinion that very serious consequences would follow if the Act were fully implemented, as it would be from 1 March 1836, when the final stage was reached, and children between twelve and thirteen were limited to a forty-eight hour week; and this opinion came to be shared by the inspectors, who at first tended to be sympathetic to the owners' point of view.[2] Against this background of dissatisfaction with the Act of 1833, two bills were introduced to change it: the first in 1835, in accordance with opinion to be found in the Ten Hour Movement, and the second, in 1836, taking account of the views of the recalcitrant manufacturers. The bill of 1835, introduced by Hindley and Brotherton, involved the repeal of the Act of 1833 and the gradual introduction over four years of a ten hour day for all under twenty-one;[3] the bill of 1836 was introduced by Poulett Thomson, President of the Board of Trade, and amended the Act of 1833 so that children between twelve and thirteen should not be limited to a forty-eight hour week.[4] But neither bill was

[1] See below, Chapter 3 (i).
[2] M. W. Thomas, *op. cit.*, p. 76.
[3] *Ibid.*, pp. 87–8.
[4] *Ibid.*, pp. 88–9.

successful. The first was overshadowed by the second, which was
an 'official' government bill; the second caused considerable
controversy, and passed its second reading by only two votes. In
these circumstances, the government decided to drop the bill, and
gave an undertaking that the 1833 Act would be enforced.[1]

In practice, however, there were considerable difficulties in the
way of its enforcement: more considerable difficulties than might
be thought from an examination of the Act's painstaking provisions. The inspectors were only four in number, and yet they
had to cover the whole country. One inspector was responsible
for an area with two thousand seven hundred factories, with about
a quarter of a million workers; it is, perhaps, not surprising that
he collapsed under the strain and had to resign in 1836, after
which a more satisfactory organisation of districts was devised.[2]
It is true that superintendents were appointed to assist the
inspectors; but their status was not clearly defined and their
powers were limited – they were not, for example, authorised to
enter all parts of factories and could be excluded by the owners.[3]
Again, the careful arrangements made for the issue of certificates
by surgeons or doctors did not always work very well. Some
doctors were rather less than scrupulous in issuing the certificates,
and they were often appealed to by parents to accept their word
that the child was of the lawful age.[4] And in the days before a
well-defined medical profession existed, there were men who had
very few medical qualifications, or even none at all, but who
posed as doctors and issued certificates to children. To try to deal
with such evasion and fraud, the inspectors attempted to establish certain criteria – such as height and the state of the teeth –
for the guidance of doctors to determine the 'ordinary strength
and appearance' of a child of nine years of age; but such schemes
were not wholly satisfactory, and ran into difficulties.[5] Further,
the check provided by the counter-signature of the magistrate was
not always effective; many magistrates were willing to acquiesce
in the issue of false certificates, and many others did not actually
see the children for whom they vouched, since this was not re-

[1] *Ibid.*, p. 93.
[2] *Ibid.*, pp. 98–100.
[3] *Ibid.*, pp. 101–5.
[4] *Ibid.*, p. 124.
[5] *Ibid.*, pp. 127–33.

quired by the Act; and sometimes, an accumulation of three months' certificates was sent to a magistrate for counter-signature *en masse*, without a child being seen by him.[1] Other evasions were by no means uncommon: certificates were lent or sold, and parents often smuggled children into factories without a certificate.[2] Again, it was sometimes difficult to convict a factory owner who was held to have broken the law. The Act did not exclude owners who were also magistrates from adjudication in such cases, and, not unnaturally, they were apt to apply the law and its penalties very lightly. There were, then, formidable obstacles in the way of the inspectors in their task of enforcing the Act, and they were soon to make recommendations for the removal of such difficulties. Two bills were, indeed, introduced on behalf of the government in 1838 and 1839 to improve the arrangements for the enforcement of the Act, but the Whigs did not show very much energy in their promotion, and both were dropped.[3] Thus in 1840, Ashley, once again active in the cause, proposed that a Select Committee be appointed to examine the operation of the Act of 1833; this was accepted, and in March 1840 the committee, under Ashley himself, set to work. It completed its task by February 1841 and made various recommendations.[4] But with the Whigs in the last days of their tenure of office, the political situation did not allow even the discussion of these recommendations in parliament, and the matter had to wait. In a sense, the decade almost ended as it began, with factory reform once again under scrutiny and examination.

Yet such a verdict would be unfair if taken to imply that little or nothing had been achieved in the course of the 1830s. Factory reform was discussed and investigated at the 'unofficial' and the 'official' level as never before; and although what was achieved was a disappointment to the popular movement, it was of no small importance. The Act of 1833 was wider in its scope than earlier acts; it applied to all the textile industries except lace, and, in certain instances silk, whereas previous legislation had been concerned only with cotton. Then again, both the commissioners and the Act dealt with the question of education for factory children and with the vital question of the enforcement of factory

[1] *Ibid.*, p. 124.
[2] *Ibid.*, p. 125.
[3] *Ibid.*, p. 146–58.
[4] *Ibid.*, pp. 175–90.

legislation. If, in practice, the Act did not always work very smoothly, it should be remembered that it was in the nature of a pioneering effort and that powerful vested interests were ranged against it. And it must also be borne in mind that the Act was by no means entirely without effect; concentration on its failures should not obscure its successes. To take one example: Ashley's Committee of 1840 reported that night work for young persons was exceptional, and this was in large measure the result of the Act. Moreover, the experience gained in trying to make the Act of 1833 work revealed the complexity of the problem and the ways in which improvements might be made; and the fact that the Act created a body of men – the Factory Inspectors – whose professional life was bound up with the effective enforcement of legislation made it much more likely than it had been previously that an impetus to improvement would be sustained.[1] In terms of the attention given to the question and the solutions devised and put into effect, the 1830s occupy an important place in the history of factory legislation.

(ii) *Poor Law Reform*

The administration of poor relief in England at the beginning of the 1830s lay in a state of considerable confusion and disorder. The basic unit of administration was the parish, as it had been since Elizabethan times. The two Elizabethan Acts of 1598 and 1601 had made the parish responsible for the relief of its own poor and gave authority to the churchwardens and certain other inhabitant house-holders – the 'overseers' – to levy a rate from which to award and distribute relief. The overseers, part-time and unpaid officials, were to be appointed annually by the county magistrates, in whom was vested the task of supervising the entire working of the system, under the general direction of the Privy Council. Thus from the late sixteenth and early seventeenth century, poor relief was administered at a local level, with only rather remote central control; and the passage of time and subsequent amendment and improvisation tended to confirm these features and, indeed, to complicate them. As the monarchy declined in power, the Privy Council left the local authorities much to their own discretion, and within the parish itself, various

---

[1] See below, Chapter 2 (iii).

other agencies came to exercise poor relief functions. The parish vestry, composed of all ratepayers who chose to attend, acquired considerable practical influence in matters of poor relief, and after 1819, it was empowered to elect a select vestry to inquire into and determine the proper objects of relief and the nature and amount to be given. Also after 1819, vestries might appoint a full-time salaried assistant to help the annual overseer in the discharge of his duties. The administration of relief, then, came to be carried out by a variety of parochial bodies and officers: annual and assistant overseers, vestries, both open and select. The arrangement varied from parish to parish; and the precise relationship between such bodies and officials as existed and the county magistrates, who retained their part in the system, could, on occasion, give rise to awkwardness and confusion. Moreover, while the parish remained the basic unit of administration, an Act of 1782 made it possible for parishes to form unions for poor relief purposes, and similar groupings of parishes were carried out by local acts of parliament. Where such unions existed, a board of elected poor law guardians was empowered to administer relief. Thus, although a certain administrative framework was in existence, there was no suggestion of uniformity or even coherence within it: rather a bewildering complex of local experiment and variation, with little or no central direction or control.

If the system of administering poor relief thus became subject to local custom and practice, the same is true of the principles on which that relief was administered; and here too, Elizabethan precepts had been modified and amended in the course of the centuries. The Acts of 1598 and 1601 had distinguished between different kinds of person who might require relief: those who were unable to find work, those who, for reasons of sickness, age or other infirmity, were unable to work, and those who were unwilling to work. The first of these – the 'able-bodied poor' – were to be set to work by the overseers of the parish on a stock of goods; the second – the 'impotent poor' – were to be assisted by the overseers, and in most cases this would take the form of money payments; and the third – the 'idle poor'– were to be punished and sent to houses of correction, where they would be compelled to work.[1] The actual physical surroundings in which these different kinds of 'relief' were carried out came to vary considerably from parish to parish. Work for the able-bodied

[1] A. G. R. Smith, *The Government of Elizabethan England* (1967), p. 80.

poor might be provided out of doors, and relief for the impotent poor given at home; but in some parishes, the former were sent to a special building where they were set to work and the latter admitted to an almshouse; and, as has been mentioned, houses of correction existed for the idle poor. Or again, and this appears to have been by no means uncommon, the same building would house all three: and this arrangement seems to have been, at least in part, the origin of that infamous institution, the workhouse, where the poor were herded together in unpleasant surroundings and the punitive aspect of relief stressed, irrespective of the causes of poverty. In the early eighteenth century, the practice of granting relief only inside a workhouse appears to have become more widespread, and in 1723, overseers were granted authority by act of parliament to build workhouses where they did not already exist, and refuse relief to those unwilling to enter them. In some parishes, this practice was retained; but in many others, outdoor relief became very common with the introduction in the 1790s and thereafter of the Speenhamland system. Faced with distress and disturbance caused by a number of bad harvests and low wages, the magistrates at Speenhamland, Berkshire, decided in 1795 that wages should be supplemented out of the poor rate by the overseers, the amount being determined in accordance with the price of bread and the size of the applicant's family. Speenhamland, however, was not a system in the sense that it was entirely uniform, for the details varied from parish to parish; nor was it by any means applied to all parishes. And there were other forms of outdoor relief in existence, such as work done for the parish and superintended by the overseers. Nevertheless, there is no doubt that Speenhamland became very commonly adopted, even if not in uniform shape, and this was particularly true of the southern counties of England. And although it had been designed to meet an emergency situation in the 1790s, there was little sign that it would be abandoned; on the contrary, it tended to spread and was especially prevalent in the years after 1815. Moreover, not only did it mean that outdoor relief became widespread, but also that persons in independent employment received that relief, whereas the former principle had been that only those not in employment should qualify for relief.

It was, indeed, the implications and consequences of the Speenhamland system which caused contemporaries most concern about the poor law. One of the strongest objections to it was its expense and the burden which it placed on the ratepayer; a burden which, it seemed, could only become heavier since the system was considered to have many attractions for both labourer and employer. To the labourer, it held out the assurance that his wages would, in the last resort, be supplemented out of the poor rate, and that any increase in his responsibilities by way of marriage and a family would be met by an increase in relief. To the employer, the system offered the prospect of paying low wages in the knowledge that these would be made up out of the poor rate at the expense of others. Even if employers paid in rates what they would otherwise pay in wages, this was still preferable to them, since rates recurred only at intervals and could be deferred, whereas wages had to be paid regularly. Given these vested interests in the continuation of the system, it seemed likely that it could only become more and more expensive and burdensome. Another common objection was that the system had a very bad effect on those who received this form of relief: that it encouraged lazy and slovenly habits in labourers because they knew that their wages would be made up, and was an inducement to early and improvident marriages and large families, owing to the increase in relief which such changes in circumstance brought about. These points were similar to the objections put forward by Malthus and Ricardo: that far from bringing relief, the poor laws simply made things worse by increasing population and putting a strain on scarce resources: and that they interfered with the 'fair and free competition of the market', which, in the view of Ricardo, should alone determine the level of wages. 'No scheme for the amendment of the poor laws', wrote Ricardo, 'merits the least attention which has not their abolition for its ultimate object'. Then again, a point which had particular relevance after 1830 was that, rather than allaying discontent, as had been originally intended, the system seemed to be encouraging it: it was in the southern counties that the Speenhamland system was most prevalent, and yet it was also in these counties that there were outbreaks of disorder in 1830.

Such criticisms, of course, came from 'official' circles: they were the views of the propertied and governing classes.[1] Individuals

---

[1] Many of them are subjected to critical examination by M. Blaug, 'The Myth of the Old Poor Law and the Making of the New', *J. Ec. Hist.* xxiii, 151–84. See also J. D. Marshall, *The Old Poor Law, 1795–1834* (*Studies in Economic History*, 1968).

like Cobbett and Owen, who urged the organisation of the unemployed in 'villages of co-operation' modelled on the latter's experiment at New Lanark, were also very critical of the poor laws; but unlike factory reform, there was – for obvious reasons – no popular, 'unofficial' movement in existence to campaign for poor law reform. So here, the initiative for reform was taken at the 'official' level. And, indeed, from 1817 onwards various parliamentary select committees had investigated the working of the system. But none produced any remedy. Complete abolition of the poor laws, as advocated by Ricardo, was more in accordance with the sympathies of these committees than the ideas of Owen; but this seemed too drastic and impractical a step. On the other hand, the Speenhamland system seemed so deeply entrenched that it was extremely difficult to change, and the existing system of administration so tangled and complex as to defy any scheme of rationalisation or reform. The prospect of fifteen thousand parishes acting almost in fifteen thousand different ways was indeed a daunting one for any would-be reformer.

Yet another attempt to review the situation was, however, made in February 1832, when the Whig government appointed a Royal Commission to inquire into the operation of the poor laws. The commission was under the chairmanship of Bishop Blomfield of London, and had a varied membership, which included Nassau Senior, formerly Professor of Political Economy at Oxford, and an adherent to Ricardian economics, who had, in fact, already committed himself to the view that the poor laws should be completely abolished. At first, Edwin Chadwick had, on the promptings of Senior, accepted the post of assistant commissioner, with the task of investigating the operation of the poor laws in a particular area; but his energy in this post earned him a place on the commission itself. It was, in fact, very largely the drive of Chadwick which led to the production of the commissions's report in February 1834, only two years after its appointment, and the report itself reflected much of his experience in the districts which he visited and many of his ideas for reform.

It was, indeed, reform of the poor laws, and not their abolition which the report advocated. The report was, it is true, extremely critical of the existing laws; it castigated the Speenhamland system for its effects on labourers and employers; it pointed to the 'moral debasement' which, it claimed, was the 'offspring of the present system': it illustrated the ways in which allowances given in aid of wages and in accordance with the size of the applicant's family, meant that 'idleness, improvidence or extravagance' occasioned no loss and consequently 'diligence and economy' afforded no gain. It is open to question how far these remarks were justified;[1] but this point apart, the commissioners did not believe that such 'evils' as they described were 'necessarily incidental to the compulsory relief of the able-bodied'; and they held that this relief might be afforded 'safely and even beneficially' under 'strict regulations, adequately enforced'. All extensive, civilised communities, they claimed, made some provision either compulsory or voluntary, for those who were in extreme necessity, and to refuse relief was 'repugnant to the common sentiments of mankind'. But, such relief was normally given only to the indigent – that is, persons unable to work, or unable to obtain in return for their work, the means of subsistence; it was not given to the poor – persons, who in order to obtain the means of subsistence were forced to have recourse to labour. Only in England had this distinction come to be disregarded, and what therefore had to be done was to draw a firm line between the indigent, who had to be helped, and the poor, who could help themselves; and to ensure that relief was given only to the former and denied to the latter. If this were done, the system of relief would perform its true function of looking after the genuine casualties of society very much better than it did under the existing arrangements of indiscriminate awards; and the able-bodied poor would be driven on to the labour market to find independent employment, thereby ending the pauperising effects of the Speenhamland system and making the individuals involved more steady, diligent and contented. Moreover, since the worker would contribute his labour in full measure, his employer would enjoy increased return and be able to pay better wages. And by thus giving relief only to the indigent and denying it to the poor, the burden of poor rates would be considerably reduced.

The way in which all this should be brought about was, in the opinion of the commissioners, to ensure that a person in receipt of

[1] Such strictures on the unreformed system have recently come under attack, and it has been argued that the report did very much less than justice to the old poor law. For development of these criticisms of the report, see M. Blaug, *op. cit.*, and also 'The Poor Law Report Re-examined' by the same author in *J. Ec. Hist.*, xxiv, 229–45. A very useful summary of these points is given in J. D. Marshall, *op. cit.*, where the assumptions of the commissioners, and the way in which they may have been formed, are also examined (pp. 43–4).

relief should have a less desirable, or, to quote the report, 'less eligible' life than that of the 'independent labourer of the lowest class'. This 'restoration of the pauper to a position below that of independent labourer' was, to the commissioners, the 'main principle of a good poor law administration'; and it was one which, as the report freely acknowledged, had already been put into practice in certain parishes.[1] The exact method of achieving this principle of 'less eligibility' in such parishes varied from place to place: it might be done by demanding work in return for poor relief on lower wages and more unpleasant terms than those offered by independent employment; or by offering relief only inside a strict and well-disciplined workhouse. But the principle was the same: 'to let the labourer find that [the] parish is the hardest taskmaster and paymaster he can find and thus induce him to make application to the parish his last and not his first recourse'.[2] This, then, was the principle which the report recommended should be adopted in all parishes and the method which it advocated was the latter of those already mentioned: the workhouse test. All outdoor relief should cease, and relief should be available only inside a 'well regulated' workhouse. By this method, relief would be given only to the truly destitute and indigent, for only they would have recourse to the 'less eligible' way of life which the workhouse offered; the poor, rather than submit to this, would make every effort to support themselves. Moreover, the workhouse test would be a self-acting one, and would automatically sort out the indigent from the poor. To quote the report:

The offer of relief on the principle suggested . . . would be a self-acting test of the claim of the applicant . . . By the means which we propose the line between those who do and who do not need relief is drawn and drawn perfectly. If the claimant does not comply with the terms on which relief is given to the destitute, he gets nothing: and if he does comply, the compliance proves the truth of the claim – namely his destitution.[3]

There was, therefore, no need for elaborate machinery to examine claims for relief, a task which had proved very difficult under the old arrangement; simply by making his claim, the claimant examined himself.

---

[1] *Poor Law Commission Report* (1834), pp. 229–32.
[2] *Ibid.*, p. 229.
[3] *Ibid.*, p. 264.

If, however, no extensive 'vetting' machinery was required, the administration of the recommended system of relief could not be left in the hands of those who administered the existing system. The report was, indeed, very critical of the existing administrative arrangements; the absence of any central control meant that the administration of relief was carried out by 'upwards of 15,000 unskilled and [practically] irresponsible bodies' and was entirely haphazard and diffuse. The report thus recommended a thoroughgoing reform of the existing system, which would ensure greater central control and uniformity of local practice, and also much improved efficiency. A central board of three commissioners should be appointed to control the administration of the poor laws along with such assistant commissioners as might be found necessary. The board should be 'empowered and directed to frame and enforce regulations for the government of workhouses and as to the nature and amount of relief to be given and the labour to be exacted in them' and such regulations were, as far as practicable, to be 'uniform throughout the country'.[1]

In poor law matters, therefore, there was to be a complete transfer of responsibility and power from the local to the central agency; from the parish to the central board, which, moreover, was to report on its proceedings annually to the government, and suggest any further legislation which might be necessary. But while the control of the system was to be centralised, the system itself should be run at the local level, although not at the parish level. The report recommended that the commissioners should have powers to bring about unions of parishes, which would be governed by boards of guardians, elected by the ratepayers on a plural scale, the number of votes depending on the size of contribution to the poor rate. These boards could appoint local poor law officials, subject to the qualifications laid down by the Commission, and the Commission might remove such officials if they proved unsatisfactory. The local unit of administration should, thus, be the poor law union; and the existing parish workhouses would become the common workhouses of the union, or, where necessary, new workhouses would be built for the union. One advantage of this system would be that different classes of pauper might be sent to different workhouses, instead of all being congregated in the one building; thus the aged and truly

[1] *Ibid.*, p. 297.

impotent might go to one workhouse, the children to another, and where there were still able-bodied males and females willing to submit to the workhouse test, they could be segregated and be sent to a third and fourth. This would ensure that each category would receive separate and appropriate treatment, and it would save expense, since existing workhouses could be used, and the workhouses supplied by a single contract at wholesale prices. But if the parish lost its individuality in these respects, it was to retain it in matters of expense. Each parish should pay out of the poor rate for the support of the permanent workhouse of the union in proportion to the average amount of the expense incurred for the relief of its poor for the previous three years, and should pay separately for the food and clothing of its own paupers.

Such were the main points of the 'official' solution to the problem of poor relief as contained in the report of the Royal Commission, presented in February 1834; and it was but a few months before they were translated into legislation in the Poor Law Amendment Act. The bill was introduced by Althorp and was on the Statute Book within a very short period. There were, indeed, critics of the bill both inside and outside parliament; it was attacked as inhuman and unchristian in its attitude towards the poor and the administrative machine which it set up was denounced as bureaucratic and centralising in its tendencies. Such opposition succeeded in limiting the operation of the Act to five years in the first instance. But the bill did offer the prospect of reduced rates and relief for many country gentry from burdensome duties; and it thus had a smooth passage through parliament. The provisions of the Act were, then, much in accordance with the recommendations of the report. They set up a poor law administration based, on the one hand, on central control, through the appointment of a central commission of three; and, on the other, on local uniformity of practice and management, through the projected poor law unions, with their elected guardians and appointed officials. Little was actually said about the principles on which relief would be awarded and distributed; this was a matter for the central commission. But the understanding was that the workhouse test and principle of less eligibility recommended by the report would be put into effect, although discretion would be allowed as to the time and exact method of its implementation, as indeed, the report had recognised would be necessary.

The commissioners did not, however, waste any time in setting about the work of organising the poor law unions. The process, which was carried out by the assistant commissioners, and begun in the agricultural southern counties, made rapid strides in the years after 1834. In the first year, 2,066 parishes were incorporated into 112 unions, and boards of guardians elected; in the second year, 5,800 parishes were grouped into 239 unions.[1] The commissioners were, moreover, well pleased with the results of their efforts, and with the application of the principle of less eligibility. It is true that they had been met with resistance and opposition, and the commissioners themselves admitted in their second Annual Report in 1836 that 'the powers of the Act and our means of carrying it into operation, have been put to the proof by every means which ingenuity could devise'. But, they claimed: 'that the pauper labourers themselves, whose interests were so greatly affected, should adopt this course was naturally to be anticipated'; and in fact, 'such persons very quickly understood the true bearing of the Act', since in many districts, 'they set themselves, without much delay, fairly and honestly to seek a livelihood by their own industry'. Further, the commissioners stated that 'many striking instances of the revival of this feeling amongst that portion of the working classes will be found in the reports of our assistant commissioners'. Although there had been cases of individual suffering involved in the setting up of the new system, the commissioners were confident that these would soon be remedied, and, indeed, that they were far fewer than under the old dispensation. The commissioners were, therefore, satisfied that the reform was having its desired effect of reducing pauperism and improving the morals and habits of the labouring population; and also that it was bringing about a considerable economy in the burden of the poor rates.[2]

It must, of course, be remembered that such comments bore the 'official' stamp; they originated with the authors of the system who were, no doubt, anxious to see it in a favourable light. Further, it should also be borne in mind that the remedies were first applied in the areas where the main evils had been diagnosed: the agricultural southern counties. Again, the initial

[1] E. Halévy, *A History of the English People in the Nineteenth Century*, iii, p. 285.
[2] Extracts from the *Second Annual Report of the Poor Law Commission* (1836), are given in Young and Handcock, 707–710.

efforts of the commissioners coincided with the propitious economic conditions of the first half of the decade, when their assumption that the 'poor' could always find work if they were only made to do so had some validity. But when the commissioners turned their attention to the northern counties at the beginning of 1837, it became clear that the conclusions reached by the report were based on insufficient evidence, and that its remedies were neither universally nor eternally relevant. The report had not, in fact, dealt adequately with the urban and industrial environment, nor had it examined the effects of such phenomena as trade cycles and technological advance; again, it had not taken account of the fact that poor relief in the north had not reached the same proportions as in the south, but was regarded mainly as temporary relief essential to survival in periods of unemployment. And it was, indeed, by harsh misfortune that one of these periods occurred at the very time when the remedy of the report was put into effect in the north, in 1837–38. A trade recession caused factories to close and resulted in widespread unemployment; the distinction between unavoidable indigence and avoidable poverty became meaningless, since no work was to be had, however anxious or willing the individual to find it. In these circumstances, it became impossible to apply the workhouse test with full vigour; there was simply not enough workhouse accommodation available for those who needed relief. The commissioners were thus forced to authorise relief in the emergency and resorted to the expedient of an outdoor relief labour test, whereby relief was given on condition that the recipient worked on a project undertaken by the local poor law union. In Nottingham, for example, this kind of test was put into effect in 1837, and relief given to those who worked on a road through property belonging to the corporation.[1]

It is true that the Act had empowered the commissioners to prescribe conditions for the relief of the able-bodied other than admission to a workhouse; and the commissioners claimed that the expedient of the outdoor relief labour test rendered the new poor law fully able to cope with industrial distress. Once again, however, these were the 'official' comments, and it is clear that the operation of the law was not as simple and straightforward as the report of 1834 had envisaged, and had to be modified in practice.

[1] Details of this episode are given in the *Third Annual Report of the Poor Law Commission* (1837). Extracts are in Young and Handcock, 711–14.

In 1841, the commissioners recognised this by the issue of a General Order on the outdoor labour test, which regularised and clarified the matter. Further, if there were departures from the strictures of the report in the case of the able-bodied poor, the workhouse test was not always rigidly applied to the aged and infirm, who, in many cases after 1834, continued to receive out-door relief. A select committee of the House of Commons in 1837–38 reported that 'it appears that relief to the aged and in-firm has been generally given out of the workhouse, and the allowances to this class of paupers have been rather increased than diminished since the passing of the law'.[1]

It may be argued that such modifications made the actual operation of the new poor law rather more humane than might be thought from a reading of the report; and more beneficent than contemporary critics were prepared to allow. Again, a recent writer, David Roberts, has suggested that the commissioners were not insensitive to the needs of those who actually submitted to the workhouse test. Conditions in the workhouses were not, perhaps, as bleak as the principle of less eligibility might indicate, and not as bad as many reports made out. Roberts has shown that there was a great deal of inaccuracy and exaggeration in the reports which *The Times* carried on the subject; and, although he admits that there were dismal conditions in several workhouses, he argues that these were the fault not of the commissioners, but of local officials who ignored or neglected the commissioners' regu-lations. 'Their regulations', Roberts writes, 'were not so very harsh. In their rules for medical care, diets, schooling, discipline, health and in their flexible application of the workhouse test, they showed a benevolent concern for the welfare of the pauper'.[2]

It would, however, be a mistake to take such arguments too far. As far as the outdoor labour test is concerned, the commissioners did not regard this as a departure from the spirit of the law. 'It must be admitted', they said in their third Annual Report, 'that indoor relief is more certain, simple and easy in its application; but the outdoor labour test is the same in principle. In both cases, a man's time is taken in exchange for his maintenance and he must be withdrawn from other modes of gaining subsistence to test the reality of his present want and destitution'.[3] Further,

---

[1] Extracts from the Report are quoted in Young and Handcock, 721.
[2] D. Roberts, 'How Cruel was the Victorian Poor Law?' *H.J.*, vi, 107.
[3] Quoted in Young and Handcock, 713.

criticisms of the conditions in workhouses cannot be wholly discounted and to talk of the 'welfare' of the pauper is hardly compatible with the principle of less eligibility, which was not directed at welfare, but at making the lives of the indigent who had recourse to relief so unattractive that the poor would not be tempted to join them. And, as Roberts admits, although physical hardships may not have been intended, certain hardships were; there had to be hardships, otherwise the whole system broke down. Some of these were, perhaps, inseparable from institutional life, such as early risings, insistence on punctuality, and segregation of the sexes; but there were others which seem unduly vindictive, like silence at meals. Thus, however nourishing the food or clean the beds, there were what Roberts calls 'psychological hardships', which, he concedes, *were* imposed to make this a 'less eligible' way of life.[1] It may thus be argued that in order to force the able-bodied to work and reduce the rates, the new poor law penalised the very people, the truly indigent, who were in greatest need of relief. Further the Act attached a moral stigma to a person's inability to work, which was to last for a very long time. The workhouse became a dreaded and humiliating institution, and in the early twentieth century, it could still be called the 'gaol as well as the goal of poverty'. It was, indeed, only in the early twentieth century that the principles of 1834 were finally replaced, although measures of social policy in other fields had in the meantime somewhat overtaken them.[2]

If the principles of poor relief embodied in the Poor Law Amendment Act were of considerable contemporary importance and held significance for the future, the same is true of the administrative system which the Act set up. This was, indeed, denounced in many quarters at the time as 'unconstitutional' and 'centralising', and such criticisms were directed at the fact that, in an attempt to keep it free from party political influence, the commission had been constituted as an extra-parliamentary body, the members of which were neither under ministerial control nor members of parliament; and further, that the commission entrenched on cherished local initiative by controlling from the centre what had previously been controlled from the locality. Again, the commission was attacked as 'tyrannical', and here

---

[1] D. Roberts, *op. cit.* 103, 107.
[2] See H. Beales, 'The New Poor Law', *History*, xv, 317-9.

objection was made to the powers which it had at its disposal: powers such as those to order the formation of poor law unions, to issue rules and regulations on every aspect of poor law administration, to confirm the appointment of paid poor law officials, and, through its assistant commissioners, or if necessary, the courts, to compel obedience from the poor law guardians. There was, it is true, a certain measure of exaggeration in such criticisms, and some qualifications are necessary. On the constitutional point, while the commissioners could issue rules to individual unions on their own responsibility, general orders had to be sanctioned by the Home Office and submitted to parliament for forty days before they took effect. Again, the commission could not be kept immune from political pressure, and its so-called political independence was brought to an end in the mid-1840s when it was replaced by a Poor Law Board, the president of which was a member of parliament and answerable to parliament; and the Poor Law Board was later, in 1871, merged into the Local Government Board. Again, as far as the accusations of 'centralisation' and 'tyranny' are concerned, the actual distribution of relief was not centralised but still carried out locally, and where unions of parishes had already taken place under local acts of parliament, the commissioners could not include these in the new poor law unions. Further, it should be borne in mind that the Act did, in effect, create a new organ of local government in the new poor law unions and the boards of guardians; and in practice – as, indeed, Roberts hinted – the guardians were not as rigidly controlled from the centre as might be thought, and, if so minded, could put up strenuous resistance to the instructions of the commission: in 1836, an assistant commissioner wrote to the central body: 'I am daily becoming convinced that neither we nor you have the power to carry the guardians beyond their convictions'.[1] Again, there were not enough assistant commissioners to ensure that a constant watch was kept on the guardians, and this became especially true in the 1840s, after the actual work of setting up the unions had been completed; between 1842 and 1846, there were only nine assistant commissioners, each of whom had to visit seventy-one unions.[2]

[1] Quoted in D. Roberts, *Victorian Origins of the British Welfare State* (New Haven, 1960), p. 117.
[2] *Ibid.*, p. 121.

Yet despite such qualifications to contemporary criticisms, the points made by the critics had some validity. There is no doubt that in 1834 parliament did delegate powers to the commission, and even if this lasted only until 1846, it was a practice which was to be very commonly adopted in the latter part of the century. Further, while the commissioners had to lay general rules before the Home Office and parliament, they were apt to get round this by issuing general rules as special regulations, which could be issued on their own authority. Again, the Act did bring about a considerable measure of centralisation; and in effecting a transfer from virtually independent and irresponsible local authorities to local authorities centrally controlled and supervised, the Act laid down lines which were to be followed by more and more public bodies as the century progressed. And although local resistance to the powers of the commission could be strong, these powers themselves were very considerable, and have been described as a 'vast accumulation . . . legislative, judicial and administrative'.[1] In all these ways, the Poor Law Commission made an important contribution to the development of public administration; it was, indeed, 'the prototype for the administrative bureaus of the future'.[2]

Poor Law reform was, then, an entirely 'official' measure, based on the report of the Royal Commission appointed to investigate the operation of the old Poor Law. How far the report presented a fair and accurate statement of its practice and administration is a matter which is open to argument; but there can be no doubt that its recommendations were highly influential on the policy adopted in 1834. And that policy, both in principle and in practical application, laid down guide-lines which were to stretch even into the twentieth century.

(iii) *The Scope and the Scale of Government*

If the Factory Act and the Poor Law Amendment Act were the two major pieces of 'social' legislation of the 1830s, they were by no means the only ones. Thus an Act of 1835 took account of conditions in prisons. Legislation on this subject had been passed before this; but the Prison Act of 1835 remedied certain defects in

[1] *Ibid.*, p. 109.
[2] *Ibid.*, p. 110.

earlier statutes. It left the running of prisons in the hands of the local bodies which had hitherto administered them; but it set up a central inspectorate to supervise their conduct and report to the Home Office. As in the case of factories, then, attention was paid to enforcement, which had been lacking in previous legislation. Again, in 1833, the Whig government granted a sum of £20,000 towards private subscriptions for the erection of school buildings, the money being distributed through the two major voluntary educational societies, the National Society and the British and Foreign Schools Society. This has been described as 'the first acceptance by the state of responsibility for popular education'; and in 1839 the matter was taken a step further. The grant was increased to £30,000 and a committee of the Privy Council set up to administer it and superintend its expenditure. With the provision of building grants from this fund, moreover, was to go the right of inspecting the schools, and two inspectors were appointed. One further instance of a 'social' measure in the thirties was the Railway Act of 1840, which vested certain powers of regulation and inspection over the railway companies in the Board of Trade; and following this, also in 1840, the Railway Department of the Board of Trade was set up. These developments marked the beginning of government regulation of railways in Britain.[1]

All these measures, then, involved some degree of government activity, regulation and control, and the creation of government agencies; and all took place in a period which has sometimes been described as one of laissez faire, when, it has been argued, the functions of government and the size of its administrative machinery – or, to put it another way, the scope and scale of government – were kept to a minimum and were indeed reduced. Such an interpretation of the mid-nineteenth century owed a good deal to the work of A. V. Dicey in his *Lectures on Law and Opinion in England during the Nineteenth Century*. Attaching great importance to the influence of 'opinion' on the course of legislation in the nineteenth century, Dicey saw Benthamism as the prevailing school of thought in the mid-century, and as the most important influence on the legislation of the period. And this, he argued, resulted in legislation which led strongly in the direction of individualism; the doctrine of laissez faire with Bentham and his disciples was, he claimed, 'a totally different thing from easy acquiescence in the existing conditions of life. It was a war cry. It

[1] H. Parris, *Government and the Railways in Nineteenth Century Britain* (1965), p. 1.

sounded the attack on every restriction, not justifiable by some definite and assignable reason of utility, upon the freedom of human existence and the development of individual character.'[1] Dicey's title for the years between 1825 and 1867 was, indeed, 'the period of Benthamism or Individualism'; and he drew a contrast between this period and the years after 1867, when he saw a considerable increase in government activity; and which he therefore described as 'the period of Collectivism'.

This interpretation of the mid-nineteenth century has, however, come under attack in the last twenty years, and many historians have pointed to the fact mentioned above: that in practice during these years, government regulation and control and the creation of government agencies were proceeding. Government was increasing both in scope and in scale. And this could take place alongside developments which went in the direction of laissez faire. Thus J. B. Brebner wrote in 1948 that 'looking back across the nineteenth century in Great Britain, it is possible to tabulate the parallel developments of laissez faire and state intervention almost year by year'. On the subject of government regulation, he wrote that it was 'always cumulative, building like a rolling snowball after 1832, whether in factories, railways, shipping, banking, company finance, education or religion. It might be halted, a chunk or two might even be knocked off the outside, but almost at once it was set going and growing again.'[2] And later in an appendix to the article he wrote of the 'scale and variety of state intervention during the years which Dicey characterised "The Period of Individualism". It is manifestly impracticable to differentiate sharply one period from another.'[3] Again, in 1956, Roger Prouty in the introduction to his book, *The Transformation of the Board of Trade, 1830–1855* made the point that although laissez faire continued to receive wide publicity in this period as a general principle or as an argument against a particular measure, in practice it was 'persistently defeated'. 'State intervention', he wrote, 'may not have been policy but it was the growing reality.'[4] Further, David Roberts, in his *Victorian Origins*

---

[1] A. V. Dicey, *Lectures on the Relation between Law and Public Opinion in England during the Nineteenth Century* (2nd ed., 1914), p. 149.

[2] J. B. Brebner, 'Laissez Faire and State Intervention in Nineteenth Century Britain', *J. Ec. Hist.*, viii. Supplement, 65, p. 6.

[3] *Ibid.*, p. 70.

[4] R. Prouty, *The Transformation of the Board of Trade* (1956), p. 1.

of the British Welfare State, published in 1960, traced the growth of government agencies in the period 1833–54 and saw the period from 1870 to 1911 as one of consolidation of what had been achieved earlier and not as an entirely new departure.[1] Similar points have been made by Henry Parris,[2] W. L. Burn[3] and G. Kitson Clark, who in his recent lectures published as *An Expanding Society, Britain 1830–1900,* has argued that the conception of 'a period of laissez faire' is unhelpful. It encourages the assumption that there was a 'consistency of outlook and uniformity of practice in ordinary people over a number of years which is not in accordance with the experience of history or the facts of nature. It suggests too sharp and complete a change in 1870, or whenever the final date is taken to be.'[4] If the phrase must be used, it seems possible, he has suggested, that it should be held that 'the period of laissez faire and the period of collectivism run concurrently like prison sentences and cover most of the nineteenth century.'[5]

In fairness to Dicey, it should be said that he did qualify certain of his comments. Thus in the period which he saw as one of individualism, he traced the makings of the later collectivism, and in this connection, mentioned the mid-century legislation affecting hours and conditions in factories. Further, he wrote that between 1830 and 1840, 'the issue between the individualists and the collectivists was fairly joined.'[6] Thus Kitson Clark has pointed out that those who talk in terms of a period of laissez faire before 1870 'are often influenced by what is, on examination, an inaccurate memory of what . . . Dicey says'.[7] Some of Dicey's critics may, then, do rather less than justice to his work as a whole by failing to take account of the qualifications which he made. It is, however, hard to see them as more than qualifications to the main line of argument; and the mere fact that Dicey thought it necessary to make them may suggest that he himself found it difficult to

---

[1] D. Roberts, *Victorian Origins of the British Welfare State* (New Haven, 1960), p. 95.

[2] H. Parris, 'The Nineteenth Century Revolution in Government. A Reappraisal Reappraised', *H.J.*, iii, 23–6.

[3] W. L. Burn, *The Age of Equipoise* (1964), pp. 132–4.

[4] G. Kitson Clark, *An Expanding Society. Britain, 1830–1900* (Cambridge, 1967), p. 162.

[5] *Ibid.*, p. 163.

[6] A. V. Dicey, *op. cit.*, p. 217.

[7] G. Kitson Clark, *op. cit.*, p. 162.

maintain a rigid distinction between different 'periods' of the nineteenth century. And the weight of recent historical opinion in this respect has been to confirm any such difficulties as Dicey himself may have encountered.

If, however, there is general agreement among historians that government regulation and growth may be traced from a date considerably earlier than 1867 or 1870, there are differences of opinion on at least two points. One is whether the process was continuous throughout the century, or whether it suffered a set-back in the 1850s and 1860s, to be taken up again later in the century. David Roberts has argued that a setback did occur at this time, and that the forces of localism asserted themselves and checked the growth of central government.[1] This, however, has been questioned by Royston Lambert, who has taken the view that no real check occurred; in a study which deals specifically with the public health movement, Lambert wrote that 'this so-called "era of localism" saw a significant increase in the extent and depth of interference by the central government and a momentous trans-formation in its nature.'[2] But of greater relevance to the present study is the other point on which differences of opinion have occurred, which concerns the forces which brought about the growth of government in the mid-century. It is, in a work of this kind, scarcely possible to deal at all adequately with the various points of view which have been put forward; but, put very simply, the difference is between those who would argue that the forces making for growth owed their origin to the ideas and writings of Bentham, and those who suggest that the reason lies in a recog-nition by various individuals of the needs of society at the time, and that this had no necessary connection with Benthamite principles. Thus, on the one hand, J. B. Brebner, in the article already cited, argued that state intervention was 'in practically all of its many forms "basically Benthamite" . . . in the sense of con-forming closely to that forbidding detailed blueprint for a collec-tivist state, the *Constitutional Code*, written between 1820 and 1832'. Moreover, he suggested that 'the architect of most of the state intervention was that bureaucrat of the purest essence, Edwin Chadwick, whom Bentham had set to work on the "Code" . . .'.[3]

[1] D. Roberts, *Victorian Origins*, p. 95.
[2] R. Lambert, *Sir John Simon, 1816–1904, and English Social Administration*, (1963), p. 606.
[3] J. B. Brebner, *op. cit.*, p. 62.

Brebner did, it is true, allow for industrialisation as a basic force making for change, but he still accorded to Bentham and his disciples a major part in shaping that change.[1] Other historians, however, have been inclined to cast Bentham and Benthamites in a much less prominent role. Prouty, indeed, did not mention Bentham at all. He wrote: 'in a society fast industrialising and urbanising, the demands made upon the Government to act in the general interest and in the interests of public welfare and safety grew more constant. The general application of laissez faire was impossible in an industrialising society. . . .'[2] Other historians have also contributed to the debate, and their views have tended to approximate either to the 'Benthamite' or the 'non-Benthamite' school of thought. Thus Parris[3] and Hart[4] have argued strongly that Benthamism and its adherents played a highly important and indeed crucial role in changes in government and administration in the mid-nineteenth century. MacDonagh,[5] Roberts[6] and Kitson Clark,[7] on the other hand, have seen these changes more in the light of an adaptation to the changing needs of society, which might, indeed, be shaped by a Benthamite hand, but which was not necessarily so shaped. And MacDonagh has pointed out that once a government agency had been created, there was a king of 'inbuilt' momentum to further growth. The enforcing officers might, for example, feel that they had insufficient powers or were too few in number; and their reports and complaints would provide the impetus for further expansion.[8]

The whole question of the growth of government, both in function and in the size of its administrative machinery, is one which clearly ranges far beyond the 1830s. Further, care must be taken not to exaggerate the importance of the decade in this respect. It is, for instance, true that the Factory Act of 1833

[1] *Ibid.*, pp. 69, 70.

[2] R. Prouty, *op. cit.*, pp. 1, 2.

[3] H. Parris, 'The Nineteenth Century Revolution in Government. A Reappraisal Reappraised', *H.J.*, iii, 30 ff.

[4] J. Hart, 'Nineteenth Century Social Reform: a Tory Interpretation of History', *Past and Present*, No. 31, pp. 39–61.

[5] O. MacDonagh, 'The Nineteenth Century Revolution in Government. A Reappraisal', *H.J.*, i, 65.

[6] D. Roberts, 'Jeremy Bentham and the Victorian Administrative State', *V.S.*, ii, 193–210.

[7] G. Kitson Clark, *op. cit.*, p. 163.

[8] O. MacDonagh, *op. cit.*, 59–61.

entailed government regulation of hours worked in factories and set up a government agency in the shape of the Factory Inspectorate to enforce this regulation; again, the educational measures of 1833 and 1839 granted government money to schools, set up a special body to administer it and appointed inspectors to see how it was spent. But it must be remembered that both of these measures were limited in scope. The Factory Act applied only to children and young persons; adults were deliberately excluded on the grounds that they were able to look after themselves. The government grant to schools was small and was given to voluntary bodies already undertaking – or about to undertake – the task of education; the government did not take upon itself the responsibility of setting up a 'state' school system. These two reforms did not, then, by any means involve a massive increase in the scope of government. And this was even more true in the case of poor law reform. Here the object was not to set up a state system of poor relief; this was indeed considered by the report of the Royal Commission, but rejected. The conclusion of the report stated that the measures which it had suggested were 'intended to produce rather negative than positive effects: rather to remove the debasing influences to which a large portion of the Labouring Population is now subject than to afford new means of prosperity and virtue.'[1] It is true that in order to achieve these 'negative' effects, the Act set up a government agency, the Poor Law Commission; in one sense, this did involve regulation and control, but it was not directed towards the assumption of vast new responsibilities. In many respects, indeed, the objects of the Poor Law Commission were laissez faire objects: to make people stand on their own feet and to free the labour market. One must, then, be careful to guard against the assumption that the 1830s saw a great increase in the scope of government or that, even if the laissez faire system was breached, laissez faire principles were abandoned; and more dubious still are ideas that the 1830s saw the beginning of the welfare state. Factory and educational reform may indeed be regarded as directed, however haltingly, towards 'welfare' as the term is used in 'welfare state'; but it is very difficult to see how the poor law can be fitted into this category. It is true that the authors of the law saw it as having beneficial effects on the labouring population; but the principle of 'less eligibility,' the purpose of which was to act as a deterrent, is scarcely compatible

[1] *Poor Law Commission Report* (1834), p. 362.

with modern ideas of 'welfare'. Finally on this point of caution, even if the administrative machinery set up in the 1830s is examined – regardless of the purpose for which it was set up – it would be a mistake to over-estimate its increase in scale. There were, after all, only four factory inspectors appointed in 1833, and only two school inspectors in 1839; further, the Poor Law Commission spoke of the desirability of a small and cheap agency.[1] The contemporary emphasis on cheapness and economy in government was one which could not be reconciled with the creation of a vast bureaucracy; and the contemporary suspicion and dislike of centralisation set limits to the scale of a central government machine.

Nevertheless, despite these qualifications, the 1830s did occupy an important place in the process of general government growth which has been considered; for it was during this decade that its beginnings can be traced in the passage of legislation which involved government control and the creation of official agencies to carry this out. Government did undertake greater tasks, as the appointment of the Royal Commissions of the decade indicates; select committees, which had hitherto been the most common form of inquiry, were found to be inadequate to deal with the issues which were raised. Further, government did assume new and greater responsibilities, even if these were still not very large; and it is part of the complexity of the situation to which recent historians have pointed that the growth in scope could take place within a system still widely regarded as adhering to laissez faire principles, and alongside other developments which went in the direction of laissez faire. And there is no question that the scale of the administrative machine was greater at the end of the decade than at the beginning; there were more agencies and more men in the government service. Moreover, once such agencies had been set up and men appointed whose whole-time employment and professional concern was to see that they worked effectively, it was likely that further growth in scope and scale would take place.

The question of the forces which caused these developments in government and administration is again one which goes far beyond the 1830s; but once more the decade is relevant to it. Factory reform and poor law reform have, indeed, been scrutinised by those who argue that Benthamism was vital to each and those who suggest that its importance should not be

[1] *Ibid.*, p. 296.

exaggerated.[1] Some of this debate, however, appears to be conducted rather at cross purposes; and it is difficult and indeed undesirable to come down sharply on one side or the other. Thus on factory reform, the Royal Commission of 1833 was unquestionably greatly influenced by Benthamism and Benthamites, as was the content of the report and bill; and this is particularly true of the provision for enforcement by a disinterested agency, the Inspectorate, which did not appear in earlier legislation or proposals. Yet it is also true that the first impetus for factory reform in the thirties came not from the Benthamites but from the Tory evangelicals and the Ten Hour Movement; and it is clear that inspection was commended to the commissioners by several manufacturers and was not, therefore, something which emerged *only* out of a Benthamite 'blueprint'. Again, on Poor Law reform, Benthamites were obviously prominent at all stages, commission, report and bill; and the content of the report and bill on such matters as uniformity of practice, central control and inspection was much in accordance with Benthamite ideas, and had never before been devised in the same fashion. Yet it is also clear that the commissioners took up ideas already in existence; the principle of less eligibility was already being acted upon in several parishes, and their plans for central control were, as they themselves said, very similar to plans used by savings banks and friendly societies.[2] In using terms like 'Benthamite' and 'non-Benthamite', then, a good deal may depend on the criteria which are set up. If the criteria of a 'Benthamite' measure are that its origin, form and content were due to Bentham and Benthamites and no one else, neither the Factory Act nor the Poor Law Amendment Act can properly be called a 'Benthamite' measure. But if 'Benthamite' measures were those which, in origin and form, owed much, but not necessarily all, to Bentham and his followers, then both of these reforms may earn the label. Perhaps the safest and most satisfactory explanation of the changes in government and administration is one which allows for as many different forces as possible; and, moreover, preoccupation with explanations and forces should not obscure the more important fact: that such changes did take place and in so doing ushered in the beginnings of the modern administrative state.

[1] J. Hart, *op. cit.*, pp. 42–3 puts the 'Benthamite' case: D. Roberts, 'Jeremy Bentham and the Victorian Administrative State' (*V.S.*, ii, 198–201) the 'anti-Benthamite' case.

[2] *Poor Law Commission Report* (1834), p. 296.

CHAPTER THREE

Reform: The Radical Response

(i) The Limitations of Reform

IT has been seen that throughout the 1830s, reform of different kinds was widely canvassed and discussed in popular and radical circles; and broad distinctions were made among working class, middle class and parliamentary radicalism.[1] Again, early in the decade, there was within the working class radical movement Co-operative and Trade Union activity which sought for direct improvements in social and economic conditions. The 'decade of reform' thus had to stand the test and scrutiny of such 'unofficial' movements; and their verdict proved to be one which pointed to the shortcomings of the decade rather than its achievements.

The earliest, most extreme and comprehensive expressions of discontent with the events of the thirties were made from the ranks of the working class radical movement. As has been seen, in 1830 this included advocates of political reform.[2] Working class support was, in varying measure, enjoyed by the Political Unions in their campaign for the reform of parliament; and an extreme working class radical point of view on parliamentary reform was put forward by the National Union of the Working Classes, founded in 1831, and composed, for the most part, of skilled London artisans. Further, there was at the beginning of the decade, a working class radical movement in existence to campaign for the repeal of the newspaper stamp duty, and thereby to ensure the spread of news and political information by means of cheap newspapers. This particular campaign did, in fact, overlap with that for parliamentary reform; for Henry Hetherington, founder of the unstamped and illegal *Poor Man's Guardian*, and a strenuous advocate of the repeal of the stamp duty, was an active member of the National Union of the Working Classes; and the *Poor Man's Guardian* became, in large degree, its press organ. But if reform which was largely political in nature had its sponsors in

[1] See above, Chapter 1 (i).
[2] *Ibid.*

the working class radical movement, so too did social reform; there were the short-time factory committees, with their allies in Tory-radical circles, campaigning for a ten hour day. Moreover, there were other working class movements in existence in 1830 which placed their emphasis elsewhere than on reform or reformism. There was the Co-operative movement, the main advocate of which, Robert Owen, had no belief in the value of political action; there was the Trade Union Movement, emancipated by the repeal of the Combination Acts in 1824–25. A notable feature of trade union activities in the late 1820s and early 1830s was the formation of large unions such as the Cotton Spinners Union of 1829; and even of a General Trade Union, with the establishment of the National Association for the Protection of Labour in 1830. At the beginning of the decade, there were, then, various groups and organisations which may collectively be described as the working class radical movement; and although they tended to overlap and intermingle, all harboured hopes and aspirations which in 1830 were set high. By mid-decade, however, many had undergone experiences which led to disillusionment and despair.

As far as political reform is concerned, the Reform Act of 1832 had not even passed before it was fiercely denounced by the National Union of the Working Classes. The objects of the National Union had included 'an effectual reform in the Commons House of the British Parliament' on the basis of annual parliaments, manhood suffrage, vote by ballot and no property qualification for members of parliament. This last point received special emphasis: 'this Union being convinced', ran one of its objects, 'that until intelligent men from the productive and useful classes of society possess the right of sitting in the Commons House of Parliament to represent the interest of the working people, justice in legislation will never be rendered unto them.'[1] Parliamentary reform was, therefore, seen as desirable in itself, and even more desirable in the light of the benefits which might be expected of it. Yet the very aims of the National Union of the Working Classes meant that, in its eyes, the Whig proposals stood condemned as totally inadequate. In September 1831, it described the bill as a 'mere trick to strengthen . . . the tottering

---

[1] Quoted in G. D. H. Cole and A. W. Filson, *British Working Class Movements. Selected Documents, 1789–1875* (1951. Paperback edn., 1965), p. 228. (Hereafter cited as 'Cole and Filson').

exclusiveness of our "blessed constitution" ';[1] and, in April 1832, as wicked, dishonest and diabolical".[2] Further, the activities of the Whig government and of the reformed parliament after 1832 did not suggest that reform had brought many benefits with it. The National Union of the Working Classes continued its agitation for an extensive re-distribution of political power. In May 1833, it advertised a public meeting in London 'to adopt preparatory measures for holding a national convention as the only means of obtaining and securing the rights of the people.' The Whig government, however, immediately banned the gathering; and when the ban was disregarded, the meeting was attacked and dispersed. The editor of the *True Sun* described this as a 'brutal attack upon the people . . . a diabolical outrage . . . The labouring classes find that the Whigs mock their miseries now, as the Tories have mocked their miseries for half a century past.'[3]

Municipal reform in 1835, moreover, did little or nothing to redeem the Whigs in the eyes of working class radicals. The measure was, indeed, very largely sponsored in 'official' circles and had a relatively tenuous connection with the working class radical movement, in which it appears to have aroused little interest. What, however, can be said is that the reform offered the working classes of the boroughs few, if any, substantial gains. As has been seen,[4] it did not enfranchise them to the extent that might have been anticipated; it did not provide for the election of non-property owners to the town councils; and in their first year of reformed life the town councils pursued policies which had little relevance to the interests of the working classes of the boroughs, and might even – in such matters as the appointment of police – be seen as inimical to them. As with the reformed parliament, so with the reformed corporations, the touchstone was still the representation and preservation of property; and the fact that this property was of the new 'middle class' variety was of little consequence to the working classes; it simply replaced one set of masters by another.

If institutional reform proved a distinct disappointment to working class radicals, the campaign to secure the repeal of the

[1] Quoted in A. Briggs, *The Age of Improvement* (1959), p. 286.

[2] A. L. Morton and G. Tate, *The British Labour Movement, 1770–1920: A History* (1965), p. 63.

[3] R. F. Wearmouth, *Some Working-Class Movements of the Nineteenth Century* (1948), p. 57.

[4] See above, Chapter 1 (ii).

newspaper stamp duty did not provide any greater satisfaction. In 1831 Henry Hetherington was sentenced to six months' imprisonment for his activities with the *Poor Man's Guardian* and in 1832, he was sentenced to a further six months for having continued the agitation on his release. This was denounced by the National Union of the Working Classes, which held a meeting early in 1833 'for the purpose of taking into consideration the gross attack of the Whig ministry on the liberty of the Press'.[1] On his release the second time, however, Hetherington kept up his campaign, which he saw as even more necessary in the light of the shortcomings of the Reform Act of 1832; he urged the necessity of an educational revolution as a substitute for the failure to achieve political rights. Others such as James Watson, John Cleve and George Harney, were also active in the movement, which, with the publication of hundreds of unstamped newspapers in the provincial towns and in London, reached considerable proportions. Each area of the country had its own distributor, although this was a perilous occupation, since the person concerned was liable to prosecution and imprisonment and a reward was offered to informers; more than five hundred vendors and distributors of the *Poor Man's Guardian* alone were imprisoned before 1834, when Lord Lyndhurst finally judged that the *Guardian* was not a paper and need not pay the tax.[2] The treatment prior to 1834, however, contrasted sharply with the leniency accorded to 'respectable' journals – for example the *Penny Magazine* – which were published under the patronage of such persons as the bishops of the Church of England, and contained 'safe' and 'proper' information; these were liable to the same penalties as the working class papers, but escaped prosecution.

The laws and their enforcement were, then, a source of bitterness to working class radicals. George Harney voiced his resentment when, in 1836 he found himself before the magistrates for the third time, on this occasion for selling an 'illegal' newspaper in Derby. He was reported by one of the 'legal' Derby papers as having expressed his determination to continue to battle:

In spite of all [the Whigs'] efforts, he declared that knowledge should be untaxed. He had already been imprisoned for selling these papers and

[1] R. F. Wearmouth, *op. cit.*, p. 64.
[2] A. R. Schoyen, *The Chartist Challenge* (1958), p. 9.

was ready to go to prison again and his place would be supplied by another person devoted to the cause. He defied the government to put down the unstamped.[1]

It does, indeed appear that it was partly the difficulty of 'putting down' the unstamped newspapers which made the Whigs decide in May 1836 to reduce the Stamp Duty to 1d.; for by their open violation of the law, the unstamped press had brought the law into disrepute. But the reduction of the duty did not satisfy the working class campaigners, who wanted nothing short of abolition. The effect of the reduction was, indeed, to reduce the price of the stamped papers, and this, along with the stricter provisions for the enforcement of the law and stiffer penalties for its evasion, meant that the unstamped press was virtually driven out of existence. The reduction was, in fact, seen by many working class radicals as a further betrayal; the 1d. duty was regarded as analogous to the £10 franchise, a figure high enough to deny the aspirations of the working classes.[2] In 1838, the *Northern Star* wrote that 'the reduction has made the rich man's paper cheaper and the poor man's paper dearer.'[3]

There was, then, evidence of strong resentment in the ranks of the working class radical movement at the shortcomings of the political reforms of the decade. The advocates of social reform in such circles were, moreover, little better satisfied. The course of factory reform did, indeed, make some headway, but not as much as the campaigners for the ten hour day wanted. There was considerable anger among the short-time committees at the appointment of the Select Committee, in April 1832, which was seen as a shelving of the bill sponsored by Sadler; and the appointment of the Royal Commission of April 1833, just when it seemed that Ashley's bill might pass, was greeted with derision as an attempt to 'whitewash' the manufacturers and delay the Ten Hour Bill. Oastler angrily asserted that the inquiry was 'a trick of the government' to save 'their dear friends the capitalists';[4] and such was his fury that an elaborate protest campaign was organised by the short-time committees of the northern counties and directed

---

[1] *Ibid.*, pp. 9–10.

[2] I owe this information to Professor Joel Wiener, The City College, The City University of New York.

[3] D. Read, *Press and People, 1790–1850, Opinion in Three English Cities* (1961), p. 97.

[4] Quoted in J. T. Ward, *The Factory Movement* (1962), p. 97.

against the itinerant commissioners. And even although the report of the Royal Commission was critical of factory conditions, its hostile allusions to the Ten Hour Movement and advocacy of only a limited curtailment of hours earned it a stormy reception. The *True Sun* considered it 'disgraceful to all parties concerned in drawing it up . . . a foul unnatural burden which ought to be publicly burnt in Palace Yard'. *The Guardian and Public Ledger* berated the commissioners' 'assurance, bombast, ignorance . . . insolence, malignity and sneaking and detested sycophancy towards wealth and power.'[1] Finally, after all the effort to secure a ten hour day, the Act of 1833 came as a bitter disappointment; many factory workers considered it a measure 'concocted in the vilest spirit of hypocrisy and evasion, vicious in its origin and designedly inefficient for practical working.'[2] The short-time committees of Ashton and Stalybridge announced that they were 'wishful to impress on the minds of the operatives and friends of an effective Ten Hours Bill, the succeeding facts – that they disclaim in [*sic*] every participation in the now existing law – that they petitioned, protested and remonstrated against it – that it was the Masters' Bill, drawn up and agreed to by "the Bit of a Cotton Parliament in Palace Yard" and it is no other than bullock-breeding Lord Althorp's Factories Regulation Act. . . .'[3] One critic put the measure in a rather wider context: 'What have we had since the Whigs passed the Reform Bill?' he asked. 'We have had nothing but cruelty and hypocrisy and this is a sample of the Liberty-loving Whigs.'[4]

Yet the Act which was seen as most inimical to working class interests was the Poor Law Amendment Act of 1834. This was the most deeply resented act of the decade and indeed has been called 'the most thoroughly detested act of the nineteenth century from a working class viewpoint'.[5] Here, of course, it was not a case of reform failing to meet expectations, but a measure seemingly designed to hurt and harm the working classes; in order to keep rates low and save the pockets of the propertied classes, the poor were to be driven on to the labour market, and, if they failed to find employment, forced back upon the hated workhouses,

---

[1] Quoted *ibid.*, pp. 103–4.
[2] Quoted in M. W. Thomas, *The Early Factory Legislation* (1948), p. 71.
[3] *Ibid.*
[4] Quoted in J. T. Ward, *op. cit.*, p. 111.
[5] A. R. Schoyen, *op. cit.*, p. 11.

quickly labelled 'bastilles'. The *Poor Man's Guardian* denounced the act as 'a murderer's death blow to the operative classes'. When the Assistant Commissioners put the law into operation in the southern counties, they were, indeed, met with outbreaks of resistance: early in 1835, there were riots in Kent and the magistrates themselves were driven into the workhouses; and there were also disturbances in Bedfordshire and incendiarism in Hampshire. But such opposition was sporadic and haphazard compared with the reaction of the northern counties to the introduction of the Act from about 1836 onwards. There, a highly organised campaign grew up to protest and put obstacles in the way of the implementation of the Act. Anti-Poor Law Associations were formed, many of which had as their core the short-time factory committees; those committees still in existence concentrated their energies on the new campaign and Oastler himself directed his attention to it with frenzied zeal.[1] Oastler, indeed, saw the new campaign as a continuation of the old, for in his eyes, the Poor Law Amendment Act was much the same as the Factory Act: simply another illustration of that adherence to the interests of capitalism and indifference towards labour which, he felt, so characterised 'the bloody, base and brutal Whigs', as he was wont to call them.

'Mock Reforms' – the phrase is that of G. J. Harney to castigate the Whig legislation of the 1830s and the sentiment was one which met with considerable sympathy among working class radicals. It may, indeed, be argued that disillusionment with 'reform' and with the activities of the 'reformed' parliament stimulated the development of the Co-operative and Trade Union movements in the mid-decade. As early as 1833, the *Poor Man's Guardian* stated that a communication received from Huddersfield gave a 'very favourable account of the societies in that town. They seem convinced from the first acts of the Reformed Parliament that little will be done to benefit the working classes, indeed they feel confident that no plan of reform can permanently benefit them, unless such as shall place them beyond the grinding influence of commercial competition, surplus capital and increasing productive powers.' After 1832, then, the ideas of Robert Owen had a new appeal. In October 1833 he suggested the formation of the Grand National Moral Union of the Productive Classes of the United

---

[1] C. Driver, *Tory Radical* (1946), p. 334 ff.

Kingdom which would include both Co-operative and Trade
Union support; and Owen's ideas also influenced the formation
of the Grand National Consolidated Trades Union in February
1834, although this was a Trade Union and did not include
Co-operative support; and Owen himself was not at first a member of it, but more a patron and adviser.[1] All such bodies stressed
the need for working class co-operation in order to win control of
their own destiny; after the formation of the Grand National
Consolidated Trades Union, the *Poor Man's Guardian* wrote of 'a
spirit of combination' which had 'grown up among the working
classes of which there was no example in former times. A grand
national organisation, which promises to embody the physical
power of the country, is silently but rapidly progressing; the
object of it is the sublimest that can be conceived – to establish for
the productive classes a complete dominion over the fruits of their
own industry.' Further, the architects of the Grand National and
other big Unions visualised a new kind of political organisation
where 'parliament' would be replaced by a 'House of Trades';
and ambitious claims were put forward for the Grand Council of
the Grand National Consolidated Trades Union. 'There are two
Parliaments in London at present sitting,' wrote J. E. Smith,
editor of the Owenite publication *Crisis* in 1834, 'and we have no
hesitation in saying that the Trades Parliament is by far the most
[*sic*] important and will in the course of a year or two be the more
influential.'[2]

Yet reality proved rather more sobering than these grandiose
conceptions. Their aspirations outran their capacity to achieve
them; the large Unions tended to be unwieldy and internally
divided. During its short life, which did not last beyond the end of
1834, the Grand National Consolidated Trades Union suffered
from these faults; and, moreover, the four major Unions, Builders,
Potters, Spinners and Clothiers, refused to join it at all. But in
addition to these structural defects, the Trade Unions of the mid-
1830s also met with external resistance from employers and from
the government. Lock-outs of workers who belonged to the Trade
Unions were frequent and imposed a great strain on their resources; and the government gave encouragement to employers
who refused to employ Trade Unionists, and prompted local
magistrates to keep a watchful eye on Trade Union proceedings.

[1] G. D. H. Cole, *Attempts at General Union, 1818–1834* (1953).
[2] Quoted in A. Briggs (ed.), *Chartist Studies* (1959), p. 13.

It was in this context that the famous case of the Tolpuddle Martyrs arose in 1834, when six Dorchester labourers were tried and transported for the offence of administering unlawful oaths in an attempt to form a Friendly Society of Agricultural Labourers as a section of the Grand National Consolidated Trades Union. The sentence incurred the wrath of Trade Unionists, directed particularly against the Home Secretary, Lord Melbourne; meetings and marches of protest were held, and a petition presented. But it was all to no avail, and before the end of 1834, the Grand National itself had collapsed.[1] Attempts at working class 'self-advancement' had proved as disappointing and disillusioning as the 'mock reforms'.

In contrast with this unfavourable and unflattering reception from working class radicals, the response of middle class radicals and reformers was more complex. Here, the political reforms cannot be said to have been a source of immediate anger or resentment. After all, the manufacturing and business interest which sought political recognition in 1830 did, in the course of the decade, receive it. The Reform Act gave the parliamentary franchise to men of substance and property, and it brought the great industrial towns of the midlands and north within the political nation. The *Leeds Mercury*, edited by Edward Baines and his son, with a wide circulation among the woollen manufacturers of the West Riding, described the bill as a 'glorious measure';[2] and the *Manchester Guardian*, the paper of the cotton manufacturers of Lancashire, announced the passing of the Act 'with strong emotions of joy and hope'.[3] The Municipal Corporations Act of 1835 was likewise greeted in such circles as a most welcome measure, taking the cause of reform a stage further. The *Leeds Mercury* rejoiced at the success of the reformers in the first municipal elections; and although these did not result in very striking changes in the social composition of the town council in Leeds, they did involve a considerably increased representation for dissenters.[4] The *Manchester Guardian* urged strongly that Manchester should be incorporated under the terms of the Municipal Corporations Act, and when this happened in 1838, it reported

[1] G. D. H. Cole, *op. cit.*, pp. 122–57.
[2] D. Read, *op. cit.*, p. 120.
[3] *Ibid.*, p. 141.
[4] *Ibid.*, p. 126. See also H. J. Dyos (ed.), *The Study of Urban History* (1968), pp. 328–31.

jubilantly that the inhabitants had taken 'the first great step towards ridding themselves of the feudal government under which they have laboured.[1] Middle-class radicals and reformers, then, had good reason to welcome the political reforms of the decade: and the way in which such measures promoted the interest of dissenters also evoked a favourable response in such circles as, of course, did the more direct legislation for dissenter relief later in the decade. Moreover, unlike working-class radicals, there was little reason why such persons should dislike the social reforms of the thirties. It is true that the *Leeds Mercury* supported a measure of factory regulation and that it carried some of the *Letters on Yorkshire Slavery* by Oastler; but this did not imply agreement with Oastler's point of view, nor agreement with the idea of a ten hour day. In its view, indeed, a shortening of the working day to this extent would result in a loss of output, higher prices and the loss of markets.[2] The *Manchester Guardian* took much the same line; a limited reduction in hours, which would not interfere with production, might be desirable, but 'to yield to the senseless and mischievous popular outcry for a reduction to ten hours would be an act of suicidal madness.'[3] In such circumstances, therefore, the failure of the Factory Act of 1833 to give a ten hour day was no cause for disappointment but rather for relief. Again, the Poor Law Amendment Act found positive favour in such circles. The *Leeds Mercury* welcomed the Act as 'one of the most important measures that has ever been submitted to Parliament'; and in 1836 expressed satisfaction with the working of the system; 'it was the result of sound principles, applied to a great mass of information obtained by the Poor Law Commissioners; and it will remain a monument to the honour of Political Economy.' It had no sympathy whatever with the Anti-Poor Law Movement and described Oastler and his fellow protesters as 'the most violent perverse and wrong-headed men that could be collected together in England.'[4] The *Manchester Guardian* likewise approved the new system and did not take its opponents seriously; the anti-Poor Law agitation, it claimed, was 'kept up only by an expenditure of the money and labour of the leading agitators'.[5]

[1] D. Read, *Press & People*, p. 146.
[2] *Ibid.*, p. 124.
[3] *Ibid.*, p. 144.
[4] *Ibid.*, p. 126.
[5] *Ibid.*, p. 145.

The reaction of the middle class radicals to the decade of reform sprang, indeed, not so much from what the decade did, as from what it failed to do. It is true that manufacturing middle class interest was 'recognised' in 1832; but this was only within an electoral system which still gave overwhelming preponderance to the landed, aristocratic interest. Richard Cobden, a Manchester calico printer, strongly developed the theme of the need to keep up the attack on that interest; writing in a pamphlet urging the inhabitants of Manchester to incorporate their borough in 1837, he reminded his readers that 'the battle of our day is still against the aristocracy'. And while the provisions of the Municipal Corporations Act in 1835, when applied under schemes of incorporation in the following years, certainly represented considerable gains for middle class radicals and reformers, this change in control of affairs at local level simply served to emphasise the continuing dominance of the old governing classes at national level. This supremacy of the landed and aristocratic interests meant, moreover, that the benefits which middle class radicals and reformers had expected of 1832 were not forthcoming. After the passing of the Reform Act in 1832, the *Leeds Mercury* had looked forward to what it called the 'fruits of reform': measures which, as it thought, could be expected from a 'reformed' parliament.[1] But, as the decade progressed, it became clear that not all of these fruits had been gathered, and that some remained out of reach. There was, for example, the question of dissenter relief, which did, indeed, make progress, but not as much as had been hoped. Again, there was the lack of attention given to the corn laws, which certain middle class radicals regarded as constituting an unfair advantage to the landed interest, or as Cobden put it, 'the Corn Law tyrants'. The question of the Corn Laws had, indeed, been raised in the reformed parliament. In May 1833, a motion was proposed to substitute a fixed duty, to be suspended in time of shortage, for the existing sliding scale; and its proposer, Whitmore explained that he had been silent on the matter in recent years partly because he felt that nothing could be expected from the unreformed House of Commons. But the reformed House rejected the motion by 305 votes to 106, and when in June of the same year, a motion was proposed for the total repeal of the Corn Laws, few members were even present in the House to hear it; it

[1] *Ibid.*, p. 128.

was defeated by 73 votes to 47. In 1834, petitions against the Corn Laws were presented from Glasgow and London, and Joseph Hume, in response, proposed that a fixed and moderate duty should replace the sliding scale; but this was also heavily defeated. In the debate on Hume's motion, the President of the Board of Trade, Poulett Thomson, a free trader, condemned the Corn Laws, but this simply reflected the fact that the matter was regarded as an open one by the Whig cabinet and did not indicate official Whig policy. Melbourne, in fact, was in favour of upholding the Corn Laws. In 1835 or 1836, the matter was not even brought up in parliament; at this point, indeed, it aroused little interest.

Scant progress was, therefore, made, and before long there were signs of impatience, especially in extra-parliamentary circles. The Sheffield mechanic and Corn Law 'rhymer', Ebenezer Elliott wrote in *Tait's Magazine*

How many more sessions of your reform Parliament can you afford to throw away? Think not, then, of His Majesty's renegade ministers. False to themselves, can they be true to you? . . . Haste then and destroy those deadly Corn Laws, ere they subvert the empire. Let every trade, from every town, one by one and again and again and again, send petitions to Parliament. Let brave and enlightened Glasgow speak again to timid and besotted Liverpool. Let awakened Liverpool shout to cowardly and goose-ridden Manchester: Manchester to London – and all together to England and the world. . . .[1]

In 1836 an extra-parliamentary body was, indeed, established in London to agitate against the Corn Laws; and this was welcomed by the *Leeds Mercury*, although it added that it was 'to the loud and persevering expression of public opinion' from the towns and villages of the manufacturing districts of Yorkshire and Lancashire 'that we are to look for any important influence on the legislature'.[2] In spite of the gains of the Reform Act and the Municipal Corporations Act, there were still in 1836, causes for middle class reformers to espouse.

The attitude of the philosophic or parliamentary radicals forms a third response to the decade of reform to be found within the radical movement. The radicalism of this group derived from an intellectual commitment to reform as a means of attacking the

[1] Quoted in D. G. Barnes, *A History of the English Corn Laws 1660–1846* (1930), p. 232.
[2] D. Read, *op. cit.*, p. 134.

aristocracy and advancing the cause of 'the People' rather than as a method of promoting any particular interest among 'the People'. The social measures – the Factory Act and the Poor Law Amendment Act – enjoyed the broad support of the parliamentary radicals; and in this, they showed their economic and social orthodoxy. Their interest lay much more in political, organic reform which would bring about a redistribution of power. Until 1835 or even 1836, there was some cause for at least mild satisfaction in their ranks. The Reform Bill of 1832 did not go nearly far enough, but the parliamentary radicals had supported the Whigs and were willing, if grudgingly, to accept their bill as a first step. Francis Place commented that *'the Reform Bills are in themselves of little value*, but as a commencement of the breaking up of the old rotten system they are invaluable'; and Roebuck felt that the bill was 'an instalment of justice . . . a stepping stone to further great improvements'.[1] As far as municipal reform was concerned,[2] the parliamentary radicals, especially in the person of Joseph Parkes, had been closely associated with the matter since 1833; and Parkes' reaction to the bill which he helped to draw up was jubilant. 'It is a smasher,' he wrote to Durham in June 1835, 'a grand point to get Household suffrage and a thorough purge of existing Corporations. . . .'[3] Even the Lords' amendments did not completely damp his spirits; he described the reform in September as 'the steam engine for the Mill built by "Parliamentary Reform". The one comparatively the shadow, the other the substance. . . .' And in January 1836, at the end of the week during which the first municipal elections were held, he wrote to Place:

This week the present . . . has fired the People in England and Wales with a real love of democratic and self-government. Far from perfect as the Corporation Act was – and reduced as was its original degree of perfection – yet it has done or rather will in its effects *do the business* and that at no distant time. The unincorporated towns will lust after and soon accomplish the destruction of their Self-Elect and the County Magisterial and Fiscal Self-Elect will next and be early mowed down by the scythe of Reform. The franchise you and I knew would do the trick and must lead to a uniformity and extension of the parliamentary franchise. . . .[4]

[1] J. Hamburger, *Intellectuals in Politics* (New Haven, 1965), pp. 121–2.
[2] See my article, 'The Politics of Municipal Reform, 1835', in *E.H.R.*, LXXXI, 673–92.
[3] Lambton Castle, Lambton MSS. 1 June 1835.
[4] Brit. Mus., Add. MS 35, 150, fos 99–100.

Municipal reform thus seemed to hold out fair prospects; and if the reduction of the newspaper stamp duty in 1836 could not entirely be regarded as a very full realisation of them, it was, nevertheless, a further partial victory. Roebuck had commented that the spread of news and political information through the press would 'teach the people to understand their rights, to stand up for what they ought to demand and to put down the aristocratical domination under which they had too long laboured'.[1] The reduction to 1d. rather than complete abolition, was, therefore, accepted by the parliamentary radicals more readily than by working class radicals; it was indeed followed by the establishment of a daily radical paper, *The Constitutional*, which put forward radical organic reforms: the ballot, shorter parliaments and extension of the suffrage.[2]

If there was much in the political reforms of the years up to 1836 which the parliamentary radicals might welcome, the reforms seemed also to hold out hopes of party gains. Preoccupied with what they saw as the basic conflict in society – that between the aristocracy and the people – the parliamentary radicals looked to a re-alignment of the political parties in parliament to reflect this: an aristocratic party opposed to reform and a radical 'popular' party to press forward with reform. In their eyes, the Tories most clearly represented the former party; and in due time, the latter would be composed of the parliamentary radicals themselves. The Whigs fitted uneasily into this pattern; they were neither true anti-reform aristocrats nor, in spite of their professions, true reformers. Parkes described them as 'founded upon no principle, but standing between two principles'; and the time would soon come when they would be forced to adhere either to the principle of aristocracy by joining – or replacing – the Tories, or to the principle of democracy by joining the parliamentary radicals. In either case, they would be driven from their present 'strange and anomolous position', as Roebuck put it.[3] Thus the Reform Act of 1832 was seen by the parliamentary radicals at least partly in this context. In their view, the Act marked the death of the Tory party; Joseph Parkes wrote that the elections of 1832 read 'the funeral service over the Tories'.[4]

[1] J. Hamburger, *op. cit.*, p. 128.
[2] *Ibid.*, pp. 129, 267.
[3] These points are developed *ibid.*, pp. 30–75.
[4] *Ibid.*, p. 123.

The most easily identified aristocratic party was thus already beaten. As far as the Whigs were concerned, their present hold on life, even if seemingly vigorous, would be short-lived. Grote wrote that although the Whigs 'will have it all their own way for the present . . . their reign cannot be of long duration'. No party 'can long maintain itself resting neither upon the aristocracy nor upon the people'.[1] They would, in fact, have to go one way or the other. If they became the aristocratic party, they would suffer the same fate as the Tories: 'We have buried the Tories,' wrote Parkes, in 1832, 'and if the Whigs will not do right, the sexton must be called out again'.[2] But if the Whigs did 'do right' they would be 'taken over' by the parliamentary radicals. Thus in 1833 Roebuck felt 'the Radicals must be in power before three years are passed'.[3]

If by 1835, such prophecies appeared to have been unduly optimistic, it was possible to regard the Municipal Corporations Act as providing further ground for hopeful expectation.[4] Although there had been certain 'dissenting' corporations, and the Test and Corporation Acts had been repealed in 1828, the unreformed Municipal Corporations were regarded by the parliamentary radicals as bastions of Toryism. Their abolition and replacement by elected town councils would lead to a wider enjoyment of local perquisites and patronage and thereby serve, in a material sense, local reforming interests. And more was likely to be involved than rewards at a purely local level, for such a change might well have a bearing on the results of parliamentary elections in the incorporated boroughs. The close association between the Municipal Corporations and the parliamentary elections in certain boroughs had, indeed, been greatly affected by the Reform Act; but even if the corporations after that date were no longer so intimately bound up with the electoral system, certain of the features which had accompanied and indeed contributed to their former influence did survive into the post-reform period. This function of the corporations, along with the corruption which went with it, was dealt with at some length by the report of the Royal Commission; and here the radicals might look for party advantage, for by destroying what they regarded as a

---

[1] *Ibid.*, p. 124.
[2] Quoted in G. Wallas, *The Life of Francis Place* (rev. ed., 1918), p. 328.
[3] J. Hamburger, *op. cit.*, p. 124.
[4] See my article, 'The Politics of Municipal Reform, 1835', in *E.H.R.*, LXXXI, 673–92.

Tory monopoly of electoral patronage, corporation reform would stamp out a source of Tory electoral corruption.

Corporation reform thus offered the parliamentary radicals the reassuring prospect of putting paid to any signs of life still shown by the Tories. 'The Corporation Bill,' Parkes wrote to Durham in June 1835, 'will be poison to Toryism'.[1] And this was a theme to which he frequently returned. Even in spite of the Lords' amendments, Parkes felt that the reform would be an invaluable party weapon. 'It must break to pieces the Tory Clique of the old Corporations,' he wrote to Durham in October 1835, 'and in the article of patronage alone make a great dent in the influence over *Parliamentary* Elections.'[2] And after the municipal election results were known, he wrote further to Durham in January 1836:

No more Tory Ministries I say . . . Certainly no Conservative majority can ever be got in a British House of Commons. *You* know that seals the fate of Toryism. You and I never thought a Tory majority could be screwed out of the Reform Bills. But this Municipal Reform is the life of what the 1832 measures was only the body. . . . At present we know of 36 once Tory now Liberal Corporations represented in Parliament by *one* Tory M.P., and about 17 once Tory now Liberal Corporations represented in Parliament by 2 Tory M.P.s. Most of these Tory M.P. gents will be chasse'ed. . . . These great results are in effect the greatest political revolution ever accomplished. I don't except the Reform Bills 1832, for they were the keys to this change, yet this Municipal Reform alone gives the vitality. . . .[3]

Municipal reform was, therefore, a great blow to the aristocratic Tory party. 'The Tories are burked,' Parkes told Place, 'no resurrection for them'. As far as the Whigs were concerned, Parkes felt that reform also hastened the day of their demise. 'The Whigs,' he wrote, 'will of course, raise their bidding with the People's growing force and demands. By concessions spurred on by the *People they* will be burked soon. They are an unnatural party standing between the People and the Tory Aristocracy – chiefly for the pecuniary value of the offices and the vanity of power. Their hearse is ordered. . . .'[4] In 1836, then, the future might still seem to lie with the 'People' and the 'People's party'; and the greater ease with which radical political ideas could be

[1] Lambton MSS. 1 June 1835.
[2] *Ibid.*, 23 Oct. 1835.
[3] *Ibid.*, 5 Jan. 1836.
[4] Add. MS. 35, 150, fos 99–100.

spread among the 'People' by newspapers – owing to the reduction of the stamp duty – might be regarded as a further step along
the same path.

All this, however, put prospects at their brightest; the rest of
the decade was to show that they had been unduly optimistic. The
year 1837 brought disappointments and setbacks both from a
political and party point of view. Lord John Russell's 'Finality'
speech of that year made it clear that municipal reform would
not, after all, 'lead to a uniformity and extension of the Parliamentary Franchise', as Parkes had hoped. The cause of organic
reform seemed dead. Further, the speech also had a bearing on the
hopes of party re-alignment. Since 1835 there had, in fact, been
disagreement among the parliamentary radicals as to tactics.[1]
Parkes had advocated co-operation between parliamentary radicals and Whigs; this, in his view, was the only practical way to
secure further reforms, and in the process, the Whigs would be
forced to align themselves with one side or the other. Other
parliamentary radicals, however, such as Place and Molesworth,
felt that this involved sinking their identity overmuch with the
Whigs and urged a more aggressive and independent policy, even
to the extent of making the Whigs resign by withdrawing support
in the Commons. This would be a sure way of making the Whigs
'take sides'; and politics would then be a struggle between 'reformers' and Tories. For Parkes, however, Lord John Russell's
speech showed that no more was to be 'squeezed' out of the Whigs,
who would, therefore, remain where they were; and yet, other
events of the year 1837 put paid to the views of those parliamentary radicals who had advocated a more independent line. There
was, for one thing, the failure of the *Constitutional*, which suggested
a lack of public support for the radical ideas which it put forward;[2]
and more important, the General Election of 1837, showed gains
for the Conservatives and severe losses for the parliamentary
radicals. If hopes of party re-alignment had ever been realistic,
they now became remote; the Tories were very much alive, the
Whigs remained in their 'strange and anomalous position'; and
the parliamentary radicals had to give up all hopes of ever forming the 'People's' party. In such depressing circumstances, the
parliamentary radicals showed signs of weariness and dejection,

[1] J. Hamburger, *op. cit.*, pp. 178–207.
[2] *Ibid.*, p. 211.

which even the decision of the Whigs to make the ballot an open question in 1839 did not dispel.[1]

Radical disenchantment with the 'decade of reform' thus took different forms and was expressed with varying degrees of intensity. From working class radicals there came condemnation of both political and social reform and anger at the failure of the Trade Union movement; middle class radicals felt cheated because their role in society had not yet been granted sufficient recognition and their economic interest not given full rein for development; parliamentary radicals were disappointed that the battle against the 'aristocracy' had yielded such limited results in political and party terms. Such distinctions as these are, of course, somewhat artificial; certain discontents were common to all radicals and too rigid lines cannot be drawn between the different reactions, which in many instances depended upon local circumstances. Yet the decade was, over all, a disappointment to most radicals and reformers, and in such disappointment lay the germs of the two great popular radical movements on which the decade ended: Chartism and the Anti-Corn Law League.

(ii) *Chartism and the Anti-Corn Law League*

The formal beginnings of Chartism dated from 1838 with the launching of the People's Charter by the London Working Men's Association, calling for further parliamentary reform by the adoption of the Six Points. The establishment of an organisation to campaign for the total and immediate repeal of the Corn Laws by a group of Manchester business men in 1839 marked the beginnings of the Anti-Corn Law League. But, as has been seen, the makings of the two movements were present before this, and while care must be taken not to read history backwards, both may be seen as a culmination of the popular and middle class reform movements of the decade; a final expression of disappointment and disillusionment with the 'decade of reform'. This does not, of course, provide a full and comprehensive explanation or history of either movement; but it may show the ways in which each was rooted in the immediate circumstances of its time.

The makings of Chartism may be traced well before the 1830s;[2]

---

[1] *Ibid.*, p. 247.

[2] The political reforms embodied in the Charter were in circulation in the late eighteenth century.

but in terms of the thirties, they were in existence before the final passage of the Reform Bill. There is a direct connection between the denunciation of the bill in 1831 by the National Union of the Working Classes and the activities of the London Working Men's Association in 1836–37, for certain individuals, like Lovett and Hetherington, were active in both organisations. Moreover, the stamp duty issue formed an intermediate stage in the process; the successor to the National Union of the Working Classes was the Association of Working Men to Procure a Cheap and Honest Press, of which Lovett and Hetherington were also members, and this Association in turn became the London Working Men's Association. There was, then, an almost unbroken history of artisan involvement in political pursuits and agitation in London,[1] which owed much to disillusionment with the Reform Act; and in the latter half of the decade, this found further expression in Chartism. Moreover, if there was this degree of continuity in London, it was also to be found in Birmingham. As early as 1833, Attwood expressed strong discontent with the Reform Act, and in May of that year wrote: 'Once more in your Countless Masses COME WITH ME'. At a large meeting in Birmingham, various speakers were critical of the failure of the government to extend the franchise and upbraided it for 'the great hostility shown to the interests of the working classes, which exceeds that exhibited by the Tories'.[2] The Birmingham Political Union, it is true, went out of existence with the passage of the Reform Act, but it revived in 1837; and thereafter – with Attwood once again a moving spirit – joined forces with the London Working Men's Association to press for further parliamentary reform. In London and Birmingham, then, both pioneers of the Chartist movement of 1836–37 onwards, disappointment with political reform formed a basis for later Chartist activity.

This was, however, only one element in the discontent and frustration which came to be gathered up into Chartism. As has been seen, the lesson of the thirties to working class radicals seemed to be that nothing could be expected from the Whig government or the reformed parliament except hostility to their interests. Opposition to further parliamentary reform, to the movement for abolishing the stamp duty on newspapers, to the Ten Hour Movement, to the Trade Union movement and support

---

[1] A. Briggs (ed.), *Chartist Studies* (1959), pp. 16–17.
[2] Quoted *ibid.*, p. 20.

of the Poor Law Amendment Act – these were simply manifestations of this basic hostility. And it merely emphasised the belief
that nothing could be achieved without a change of rulers, such as
a radical reform, along the lines of the Charter, would achieve.
Thus, in 1837, 'An Address to the Reformers on the Forthcoming
Elections' issued by the London Working Men's Association
traced 'most of our oppressive laws and institutions' to '*one
common source* – EXCLUSIVE LEGISLATION'; realising this,
it went on, the people '*have their minds intently fixed on the destruction
of this great and pernicious monopoly*: being satisfied that while the
power of law making is confined *to the few*, the excessive interests
of the few will be secured at the expense of the many'.[1] And also in
1837, a petition from Birmingham ran:

Your present petitioners feel compelled to declare that . . . Reform . . .
has most grievously disappointed the hopes and expectations of the
country. After five years of patient trial your petitioners have no reason
to believe that the wants and interests of the industrious classes are better
understood, or their rights and liberties better protected now, than they
were in the unreformed Parliament; and your petitioners are convinced,
that it is absolutely necessary to effect a further and much more extensive
Reform of the Commons House of Parliament before the industrious
classes can hope to enjoy any permanent relief and protection. . . .

Later in the petition, the Poor Law was singled out for special condemnation; the law which visited 'poverty as a crime' as it put it,
and accumulated 'punishment and degradation as well as misery
upon the heads of the poor'.[2] The Poor Law was, indeed, a
potent influence in drawing men into Chartism; under the force-
ful personality and leadership of O'Connor, the Anti-Poor Law
Movement in the North of England was merged into the Chartist
movement, even if in the process, certain Tory-radicals like
Oastler, who had no sympathy with the political radicalism of
Chartism, were left behind.[3] The newspaper, which in some sense
became the mouthpiece of Chartism, the *Northern Star*, began as
an organ in the struggle against the Poor Law and only later
transferred its energies to Chartist agitation. The political programme of Chartism thus derived not only from frustration at the
limitations of the Reform Act, but also from the belief that only a
parliament elected on the basis of the Six Points would bring

[1] Cole and Filson, p. 348.
[2] *Ibid.*, pp. 349–50.
[3] C. Driver, *Tory Radical* (1946), pp. 398–401.

about any relief from the burdens which the events of the decade had heaped upon the working classes.

Further, the faith which the Chartists placed in a political solution to varying problems was due partly to the failure of other methods in the mid-thirties, in particular Trade Unionism. Disappointment over parliamentary reform in 1832 did not lead to a massive re-direction of working-class energies to Trade Unionism; the movement was in existence before the 1830s and individuals like Lovett and Hetherington were almost continuously active in primarily political pursuits throughout the 1830s. Yet, as was mentioned earlier,[1] disillusionment with the Reform Act did stimulate interest in Trade Unionism; and Lovett, despite his political preoccupations, was to be found associated with it. He was Secretary of the National Committee of Protest set up after the Tolpuddle Transportation in 1834, and members of the Committee were also active in Chartism later in the decade.[2] Further, the failure of Trade Unionism did have the effect of stressing the need for political action. Henry Hetherington on a visit to Leeds in 1834 after the Trade Union efforts there had come to nothing reached the conclusion that only universal suffrage would break the workers' chains.[3] The political emphasis of Chartism may, therefore, be seen in the light of the failure of Trade Unionism in the middle years of the decade.

The makings of the Anti-Corn Law League – as those of Chartism – may be discerned before the opening of the 1830s; the Corn Laws had been subjected to criticism ever since their enactment in 1815. But what gave added point to such criticism was the failure of the reformed parliament, even with its recognition of manufacturing and business interests, to make any headway in the matter. The men who took the initiative in founding an Anti-Corn Law Association in Manchester in 1838 were local business men of reforming ideas: Thomas Potter, a wealthy cotton merchant, George Wilson, a starch and gum manufacturer and Richard Cobden, a Manchester calico printer, albeit of rural origins. And the same men were to play a very influential role in the Anti-Corn Law League founded in March 1839, which was a federation of various local anti-Corn Law Associations, with its headquarters at Manchester. The

[1] See above, Chapter 3 (i).
[2] A. Briggs (ed.), *Chartist Studies* (1959), pp. 14–15.
[3] *Ibid.*, p. 14.

formation of the League was, thus, a reflection of the feeling of many middle-class radicals and reformers that such an extra-parliamentary body was necessary to bring pressure to bear on the legislature which, they felt, was still dominated by the old aristocratic interests and unsympathetic to the manufacturing interest.

It was not, however, only secular grievances and frustrations which lay behind the anti-corn law campaign; for religious grievances were also present. In spite of the gains made by the dissenters in the thirties, many were resentful that more had not been achieved; the payment of Church rates, for example, remained a major source of irritation, which the Whigs' scheme to amend – in itself unsuccessful – did nothing to remove. Towards the end of the thirties, therefore, dissent tended to become more extreme and militant in its attitude, and found expression in various organisations such as the Church Rates Abolition Society of 1836, and the Religious Freedom Society of 1839, which called for the separation of Church and State.[1] And some of this anger and frustration – if the rather more extreme manifestations of it – was channelled into the anti-corn law movement. As Norman McCord has put it: 'Many Dissenters would be very willing to rally to an attack on the Corn Law, which was for them an attack on the parson's tithes and a wonderful opportunity to show the Established Church as the thief of the poor man's bread'.[2] In such discontents, then, lay the source of much of the support which many dissenters gave the League; support which the League was to turn to good advantage as affording its efforts a certain moral and religious sanction.

The discontents and frustrations of the 1830s were, therefore, the material out of which Chartism and the Anti-Corn Law League grew. Yet such discontents were felt only by relatively few 'activists' and more than their efforts were required to make Chartism and the League truly 'popular' movements. It was the onset of the economic depression in the late 1830s which did most to bring this about. In the circumstances of economic and social dislocation and distress caused by the depression, the grievances of the decade assumed a sharper edge; and the Chartist remedies and that of the League had a wider appeal. Attwood had indeed foreseen such a development when he wrote: 'Men do not gener-

[1] N. Gash, *Reaction and Reconstruction*, p. 75.
[2] N. McCord, *The Anti-Corn Law League* (1958), p. 26.

ally act from abstract principles, but from deep and unrewarded wrongs, injuries and sufferings. The people of England never came forward to advocate the abstract principles of Major Cartwright ... but when their employment and wages were gone ... the borough managers were quickly cashiered. Now when the next opportunity comes, a further reform of Parliament will be a much quicker and easier operation'.[1] His prophecy was accurate to the extent that it was in the context of the business depression that the Birmingham Political Union revived in 1837; its political remedies, which became merged with Chartism, certainly sought to undo the harm alleged to have been done since 1832, but they also had a special relevance to the needs of the moment. Further, as has been seen, much of the appeal of the Anti-Poor Law movement – which likewise merged into Chartism – was due to the onset of the depression at the very time that attempts were being made to introduce the Poor Law to the North of England. Again, the change from Trade Union to Chartist activity was partly the result of the coming of an economic climate which was unfavourable to Trade Unionism. If, then, the material for Chartism had been present long before 1838, it was the economic depression which released the full potential of that material. And this was also true of the League. The economic crisis gave weight to the arguments of those who had been pressing for Corn Law repeal and greatly increased the appeal of the League. The Corn Laws were singled out by the Leaguers as the most serious of the restrictions on trade, which, they claimed, caused economic depression. For, as they argued, the exclusion of foreign grain from Britain made foreign countries less able and willing to take British manufactured goods; repeal of the Corn Laws would be followed by a great expansion of commerce. The primary producers would willingly exchange their food and raw materials for British manufactured goods and unlimited markets would be opened up to British manufacturers and exporters. Trade would flow in natural channels, unaffected and un-deflected by restrictive interference; and the economic slump would find a speedy remedy.

The economic depression and its attendant social ills thus finally transformed the grievances of the 1830s into Chartism and the Anti-Corn Law League. The two movements, of course,

---

[1] A. Briggs (ed.), *Chartist Studies* (1959), pp. 20-21.

proved to be very different in style and character and numerous points of contrast may be made between them. Thus Chartism betrayed its origins and was diffuse and localised; many grievances – which might well differ according to trade or locality – took men into Chartism, and the adoption of a common political programme, even if a striking achievement, did not mean that these grievances lost their identity. The movement suffered from clashing personalities; there was little in common between Lovett and O'Connor and, indeed, considerable personal antipathy between them. Again, there was little agreement as to methods to be adopted. The distinction often made between 'moral force' and 'physical force' Chartists suggests too rigid and over-simplified a difference as to methods; but difference there certainly was between those who were inclined to favour peaceful, persuasive and long-term methods and those who wanted immediate results, if need be by force.[1] Further Chartism had little in the way of organisation and few funds at its disposal, and it appealed to the distressed sections of the community, who had least money to spare to finance its efforts. By contrast with all this, the League emerges in a favourable light. It derived from a more limited grievance; that grievance, moreover, could be met by a single legislative enactment and did not depend on the fulfilment of a programme of radical political reforms, which, even then, was envisaged as a first step to further social improvement. Again, the aim of total and immediate repeal was strictly adhered to; and attempts to widen the aim did not receive the official backing of the League, which was firmly and effectively led by Richard Cobden. There were, it is true, certain differences of opinion as to the methods to be adopted; thus when the League decided to fight parliamentary elections, this was not to the liking of all its members. But when the decision had been taken, it was followed through with determination, single-mindedness and no little skill in the art of exploiting the electoral system. Further, largely under the hand of George Wilson, the League developed an extremely efficient organisation and could draw on very considerable funds, which was partly a reflection of its appeal to the manufacturing interest and partly a result of its own fund-raising efforts. Whereas, then, Chartism tended to be a snowball of protest movements with little coherence beyond an often nominal allegiance to six points,

[1] F. C. Mather, *Chartism* (Historical Association Pamphlet, G61), p. 17.

the League was a highly organised pressure group directed to the single aim of total and immediate repeal.[1]

The difference between the two movements may thus be easily discerned and to some degree traced to their origins. Further, the fact that the movements developed separately and were on the whole antagonistic to each other may also be related to earlier events of the decade, and to events before the decade. In terms of the thirties, however, it may be argued that the experiences of these years strengthened a working-class consciousness which had been forming since the 1790s and which found final expression in Chartism; and likewise reinforced a developing middle class consciousness, which found an outlet in the League; and that these class tensions kept the two movements apart. Thus to working class radicals, the seemingly deliberate limitations of the reforms and the resistance with which Trade Unionism was met suggested that the working classes were being singled out for harsh treatment by the ruling classes; and their disillusionment was made the more acute by the common impression among working class radicals that the ruling classes were composed of the middle classes. The feeling was that the working classes had assisted the middle classes to power in 1832 and had been betrayed thereafter; thus Bronterre O'Brien, a relentless critic of the legislation of the decade, wrote in 1836: 'Previously to the passing of the Reform Bill the middle orders were supposed to have some community of feeling with the labourers. That delusion has passed away . . . it vanished completely with the enactment of the starvation law [*i.e.* the Poor Law]. No working man will ever again expect justice, morals or mercy at the hands of a profit-mongering legislature'.[2] This impression that the middle classes were identical with the ruling classes was, of course, an illusion; yet illusion can be as powerful as reality and it may be held that in this case it helped to strengthen class consciousness among working class radicals. Again, the Trade Union movement of the early and mid-thirties may be interpreted as an attempt by working class radicals to control the destiny of their class by economic union; and when this failed, the establishment of the London Working Men's Association in 1836 as an attempt to further working class interests by united working class political action. Chartism may thus be

[1] See N. McCord, *op. cit.*, *passim*.

[2] Quoted in E. P. Thompson, *The Making of the English Working Class* (1963, Pelican edn., 1968), p. 904.

seen in this light: a manifestation of working class consciousness; an attempt by the working classes to 'go it alone', without help from any other class which might betray them yet again. And the Chartist years may be regarded as the outcome of the period of 'the making of the English working class', when 'common institutions, programmes, forms of action and modes of thought'[1] were finally discovered. As far as the middle classes were concerned, it may be argued that the effect of the reforms of the decade – in particular the political reforms – had been to mark them off from the working classes on the one hand and yet still to keep them apart from the aristocratic ruling classes on the other; and that in this situation, a middle class consciousness was engendered, finding its means of expression in the League.[2]

Such an interpretation, however, would not be without its critics. They might well argue that to generalise about working class feeling and opinion is to ignore the considerable differences within the working classes, which might vary according to trade or locality; that men still thought of themselves as members of particular trades with particular grievances rather than as members of the working class with working class grievances; and that, in particular, a considerable gulf existed between 'artisans' and 'labourers'.[3] In support of such arguments, it could be pointed out that Trade Unionism in the mid-decade did not command complete working class support; and that Chartism could scarcely be held to illustrate working class unity and might even be held to illustrate the reverse. Further, co-operation with other classes was not by any means ruled out by all working class radicals. Parliamentary radicals, such as Francis Place, played a part in the establishment of the London Working Men's Association[4] and the procedure of petitioning parliament favoured by so many Chartists, and adopted on three occasions, presupposed that certain members of parliament – even if they belonged to a different class – would not be unsympathetic to their cause.[5] Further, there was nothing incompatible between Chartist political aims and the total and immediate repeal of the Corn Laws canvassed by the

[1] *Ibid.*, p. 937.

[2] A. Briggs, 'Middle Class Consciousness in English Politics, 1780–1846', *Past and Present*, No. 9. pp. 65–72.

[3] R. Currie and R. M. Hartwell, 'The Making of the English Working Class?' *Ec.H.R.*, xviii, 638.

[4] D. J. Rowe, 'The People's Charter', *Past and Present*, No. 36, pp. 73–86.

[5] F. C. Mather, *op. cit.*, p. 22.

League; both were long-standing radical demands. And hostility between Chartism and the League was not a permanent and unchanging feature of relations between the two movements, but was confined only to the years 1839–41.[1] On the question of middle class consciousness, it might be conceded that this was better developed than working class consciousness and that the League was a vehicle for it. But even here there are clear dangers in generalisations; the League ran into considerable apathy from sections of the middle classes and the pronouncements of the *Leeds Mercury*, or any other paper, are evidence of the views of that particular paper, but not necessarily those of the middle class. And within the League, there was a desire to win working class support for repeal, which would suggest a desire for class collaboration. Finally, it can be held that both movements were much too intricate to be explained in class terms, and the society out of which they arose too amorphous to be amenable to class distinctions and categories.

The whole question of class, class consciousness and class relationships is an extremely complex one. As with other matters, much may depend on the definition given to the words: whether a rigid definition, resting on complete solidarity and cohesiveness of interest and purpose is required, or a rather looser definition is accepted – such as that urged by E. P. Thompson – which sees class as something which 'happens when some men, as a result of common experiences (inherited or shared), feel and articulate the identity of their interests as between themselves, and as against other men, whose interests are different from (and usually opposed to) theirs'.[2] If the former definition is applied, Chartism cannot qualify as a class movement; the League, on the other hand, has rather better credentials. If the latter and looser, more subjective, definition is taken, both have qualifications. For consciousness of common interests, if by no means all-pervasive, was present in both movements; and so too was awareness that these were separate from other interests. Militant working class consciousness was evident in Chartism; and militant middle class consciousness in the League;[3] and the two movements reacted on each other to strengthen this consciousness, which, especially in the case of the League, was made the sharper by the awareness

[1] *Ibid.* See also A. Briggs (ed.), *Chartist Studies* (1958), pp. 342–71.

[2] E. P. Thompson, *op. cit.*, pp. 9–10.

[3] A. Briggs and J. Saville (eds.), *Essays on Labour History* (1960), pp. 59–69.

among its members of the entrenched privileges of the landed,
aristocratic classes.

The origins of Chartism and the Anti-Corn Law League were,
therefore, present throughout the 1830s, but it required the
economic depression of the late thirties to develop these and
transform them into two popular movements. And once they
had developed into such movements, they never entirely lost the
stamp of their origin. Their 'class nature' may also be traced to
earlier events and experiences, although this was strengthened
and sharpened once the movements had gathered strength and
were in existence side by side. The strongest expression of radicalism at the end of the decade was then to be found at the popular,
or, it may be argued, class, level; and by contrast, parliamentary
radicalism suffered decline and virtual eclipse.

(iii) *The Demise of the Parliamentary Radicals*

At first sight, it might seem likely that the emergence of Chartism
and the Anti-Corn Law League would have been greeted with
enthusiasm by the parliamentary radicals, for both movements
put forward aims which had long been canvassed in parliamentary
radical circles. The organic reforms contained in the Charter were
precisely what the parliamentary radicals wanted, and, indeed, to
Francis Place the Charter was 'the general and all comprehensive
measure'.[1] Again Corn Law repeal was a cause which had attractions for many parliamentary radicals, and this was especially
true in the political situation of the late thirties. The corn laws
were regarded by the radicals as symbols of aristocratic privilege
and exclusiveness, and their repeal seen as certain to administer
a further sound blow to the *ancien régime*: a prospect which was
entirely welcome and heartening. And an attack on the corn laws
in the late thirties would serve as a good weapon with which to
belabour the Conservatives, so alarmingly showing signs of life
when the radicals thought them safely dead and buried. The
Conservatives could be expected to rally to a defence of the corn
laws and this would force them to sponsor a cause which went
against the general direction of economic thought and practice
towards free trade. The Conservative party could thus be
branded as the party of the exclusive, aristocratic interest holding
on to the corn laws and thereby, it could be argued, keeping the

[1] J. Hamburger, *Intellectuals in Politics*, p. 74.

price of food high.[1] Repeal, then, held out hopes of political advantage and party gain. Chartism and the League might thus seem to offer everything the parliamentary radicals had long cherished and yearned for.

Yet while there was a great deal of common ground between the aims of Chartism and the League and those of the parliamentary radicals, there were certain obstacles in the way of a united effort. Certain of the social grievances which went to make up the Chartist movement were not felt by the parliamentary radicals; there was, indeed, a measure of support for the principle behind the Poor Law from individuals like Francis Place. Further, Chartism smacked too much of violence for the liking of the parliamentary radicals. If they themselves had threatened and talked of violence in 1831–32,[2] it seems unlikely that this was more than a tactical device. With certain of the Chartists, however, it was not just 'talk' or 'tactics'; it might be – and on occasion was – put into effect.[3] And any large scale outbreak of Chartist violence was scarcely likely to spare the parliamentary radicals. Again, as far as the Anti-Corn Law League was concerned, it was felt by many parliamentary radicals that it was too obsessed with the one end and object of repeal, to which Cobden adhered with unbending insistence. The parliamentary radicals were more inclined to see corn law repeal as part of a general drive towards further organic reform. Parkes, it is true, assisted the League in its electoral activities, drawing on his great experience of such matters; but he complained that the Leaguers were 'men with one idea' who threatened 'the general Liberal cause by sacrificing it at the shrine of their single question. A one-eyed horse can see better than these Manchester gents'.[4] He saw the campaign for repeal in a wider context.

I plainly see that the Anti-Corn Law question is the fanaticism of the day [he wrote in 1841] If Peel staves off the Question – and he cannot practically settle it without shivering his 'Conservatives' to pieces – he will be agitated to death. . . . The agitation of the fanaticism of the day is only commenced. If not yielded to, it will again assault the representative system. I see the storm brewing in the talk of Cobden & Co. They are the

---

[1] N. McCord, *op. cit.*, pp. 20, 22–3.
[2] See above, Chapter 1 (i).
[3] J. Hamburger, *op. cit.*, p. 253.
[4] *Ibid.*, p. 188.

Tom Attwoods of 1831–32. The outdoor men have always scattered the Tories and always will. . . .[1]

But most parliamentary radicals were less confident than Parkes that the campaign for the repeal would, in fact, lead to further organic reform. Place regarded repeal as a 'very momentous measure though only one of detail'; and John Stuart Mill wrote that the only way to get rid of the corn laws was 'to agitate not against the Corn Laws, but against the source of the Corn Laws, as well as of every other grievance – the vicious constitution of the legislature'.[2]

The parliamentary radicals thus had difficulty in accommodating their views and conduct to either movement. And the very fact that there were two movements, each with strong class overtones, tended to contradict and undermine all their ideas that a radical party would come into being, based on the whole People. The existence of Chartism and the League, and the hostility between them, showed the divisions and conflicts among the 'People'; a 'People's Party' could not, therefore, emerge. The parliamentary radicals recognised that class differences existed, but wanted to bring about a 'juncture of the middle and working classes', as Place put it, in order to bring pressure to bear on the aristocracy, who remained the great enemy. Chartism and the League at once reflected and accentuated class tensions and these made such a 'juncture' impossible; thus both movements, and in particular Chartism, came in for criticism from the parliamentary radicals. Place delivered scathing judgments on the leaders of the Chartist movement, whom he saw as 'misleaders of the people': Stephen was a 'malignant, crazy man', O'Brien 'a three parts insane and savage man', Hetherington an 'honest man, with too little brains to guide him', and O'Connor 'the most reckless of them all', who 'knew that he could only hold the people to himself by increasing the enmity between the working and all other classes of the people'.[3]

Thus at the end of the decade, the parliamentary radicals were a rather sad and dejected group. In spite of all the reforms, the Tories were still an active force in politics and were indeed becoming the major political force. The Whigs, if in decline,

[1] National Library of Scotland, Ellice MSS. (not yet permanently catalogued) 16 Sept. 1841.
[2] J. Hamburger, *op. cit.*, p. 74.
[3] *Ibid.*, p. 254 ff.

were still in existence, and had fused their identity neither with the Tories nor with the People. The People themselves – the source of all hope – had taken on flesh and blood in the form of Chartism and the League. Political realities thus refused to conform to the abstractions of the parliamentary radicals; and deprived of satisfaction in politics, and squeezed off the political stage, most turned for solace to scholarship and intellectual pursuits: politics, as Mrs. Grote put it, were 'dead and buried', and 'desiring to mix no more therein we relapse into letters, Philosophy and projects for rational enjoyment of our lives . . .'[1] They had learned the lesson that politics are, perhaps, seldom as rational as intellectuals consider they ought to be.

[1] *Ibid.*, p. 267.

CHAPTER FOUR

Reform: The Legacy

THE immediate legacy of the 1830s lay in what reform had failed to achieve rather than in what it had achieved. Chartism and the Anti-Corn Law League were both manifestations of this failure; and both also evidence of the social and economic problems in existence at the end of the decade to which certain reforming measures – in particular the Poor Law – had contributed. Peel and the Conservative party coming to office in 1841 were, then, the heirs to this legacy; a legacy of political frustration, social grievance, class bitterness, economic dislocation, radical protest.

A full consideration of the way in which the Peel ministry was to handle this situation lies outside the scope of this study.[1] Suffice it to say that it was not in the direction of further extensive reform in State and Church, nor in the sponsoring of social reforms. Rather, Peel saw the solution as consisting in the freeing of the business and commercial interest from restrictions – especially trading restrictions – so that the economy would expand and go on expanding virtually of its own accord. This would eliminate depressions and slumps, which brought with them business failures, unemployment and distress; the creation of favourable conditions for economic expansion would, indeed, be a stimulus to greater prosperity in which all classes would share, and which would thus blunt the edge of radical protest. It was in this spirit that Peel framed his free trade budgets, the most notable being in 1842 and 1845; and the repeal of the Corn Laws in 1846 was essentially a continuation of this policy and not a sudden conversion because of the Irish famine nor a surrender to the Anti-Corn Law League.[2] It was a policy which was to prove successful; and while it was by no means entirely responsible for the increase in economic well-being and social harmony which marked the late 1840s and 1850s, it certainly contributed to this improved state of affairs. But the price to be paid was the break-up of the

[1] See N. Gash, *Reaction and Reconstruction*, pp. 148–52.
[2] B. Kemp, 'Reflections on the Repeal of the Corn Laws', *V.S.*, v, 189–204.

Conservative party. Part of the reason for this lies in the fact that the Conservative party in the 1830s had been built around constitutional and religious questions; the questions raised by reform in State and Church. But once in office, it had to face different issues – issues which were in large measure social and economic. Peel and his ministry were able to adjust to the new circumstances; and indeed, Peel always claimed that his policy between 1841 and 1846 was entirely in the 'conservative' interest; that it would save the traditional ordering of society from exposure to radical criticism and attack and thereby perpetuate it; and that it was, therefore, a logical continuation of his policy of the thirties. But it proved difficult to convince the rank and file of the party that it should be concerned with economic and fiscal reforms; in their view, its purpose remained to defend the institutions of State and Church; and the mere fact that a Conservative government was in office saw to that. The party born in the thirties, then, had to grow up in the forties and face its different problems; and the strains and tensions which this involved were seen to the full in 1846 when it finally split over corn law repeal.

If, however, the immediate legacy of the 1830s lay in the limitations and failures of reform, the decade also left a more positive and substantial legacy. Reform in State and Church, was, in fact, a very considerable achievement. Institutions which had lasted for centuries in much the same form were subjected to change and adjustment; and even in the short term, this made them better able to withstand radical assaults which otherwise might possibly have overwhelmed them. Thus one reason for the failure of Chartism is that the Reform Act of 1832 had already met – if only in part – the political aspirations of the most powerful campaigners for parliamentary reform. And in the longer term, reform in State and Church has been a process which has gone on ever since the 1830s, although the process has not, of course, been continuous. But all the arguments which were used against the unreformed parliament and the electoral system before 1832 could, in time, be used against the reformed; that they were, for example, out of date and did not take sufficient account of changes in society. Thus although the progress of parliamentary reform has been a slow one, its advance may be seen in the subsequent Reform Acts of the nineteenth and twentieth centuries; and its progress may well still be incomplete at the present time, when consideration is being given to lowering the age of voting and an inquiry set on foot into the institutions of government. The same points could also be made of the reform of local government. Again the process has been a slow one; this has been true of borough government and even more true of county government, which had to wait until 1888 for reform. But the Municipal Corporations Act did show the way; and the present inquiries of a Royal Commission suggest that further reform may well be forthcoming. Church reform and relief of dissenters' grievances have similarly had a long history; and while the latter has been achieved, even yet churchmen are concerned with the question of whether the Church is sufficiently 'up-to-date' and is meeting the needs of the present situation in terms of the distribution of churches and clergy. When such long-term developments are being considered, care must clearly be taken not to exaggerate the contribution of a particular period; but there can be no doubt that the legacy of the 1830s is a considerable one in the example which it set.

A similar case can be made for the decade with regard to reforms which touched on the question of 'government and society'; and here the points which have already been made should be borne in mind. That there has been a change in public attitudes to social policy since the 1830s is clear and obvious. The laissez faire assumptions which were to be found in the Factory Act of 1833 are long since dead; and the spirit which informed the Poor Law Amendment Act of 1834 is not the spirit which informs the modern welfare state. But, as has been seen, the beginnings of the modern administrative state may be discerned in the government agencies set up in the 1830s; and while there is room for argument whether such beginnings have developed continuously since then, there is no doubt that their development has been in the direction of very considerable growth. Even yet, politicians argue whether the size of the government machine is too great. Further, the establishment of a civil register of births, marriages and deaths was, in time, to provide the statistical basis for much social policy.

Finally, the political and popular movements of the 1830s had significance for the future. The decade saw the early stages in the evolution of party organisation. And if the fate of the Conservative party was to be broken asunder in the mid-forties, the Tamworth Manifesto has claims to be regarded as the foundation document of modern Conservatism, and Peel as its founder; Peel indeed has stronger claims in this respect than Disraeli to whom the credit is often given. Further, the radical movements of the 1830s struck a remarkably modern note. The 'Six Points' did not originate with Chartism, but they were brought together as its programme in a way which had not been done before. It is a commonplace to observe that the majority of these points have since been put into effect, but such an observation simply illustrates the way in which Chartism foreshadowed the future. Further, while this study has tended to see Chartism in the context of its immediate circumstances, the movement may also be approached, if rather tentatively, in the light of its contribution to later radical and working class political activity. The Anti-Corn Law League likewise did not have a new cause to champion and it went out of existence after repeal. But it set an example of a highly developed pressure group and its methods of persuasion and propaganda have been adopted by later organisations of a similar kind. And the parliamentary radicals may in some respects be regarded as the forerunners of the Fabians; although this particular connection should not be overstrained.

The 1830s in England were, then, a decade touched at many points by reform. Reform had its effects on the country's institutions and social problems; it influenced its political and constitutional history; it shaped its administrative processes and popular movements. And if in the short-term, the limitations of reform were more apparent than its achievements, the events of the decade set a direction and pointed a course which later generations were to follow and even yet pursue.

Select Bibliography

ALL general histories of the early and mid-nineteenth century – such as
E. L. Woodward, *The Age of Reform, 1815–1870* (Oxford, 2nd edn., 1962)
and A. Briggs, *The Age of Improvement* (1959) – contain information which
is relevant to the themes of the 1830s explored in this book. The best
single volume devoted simply to the decade and dealing with all its
aspects is E. Halévy, *A History of the English People in the Nineteenth Century*
(first published in English, 1927), III, the title of which is 'The Triumph
of Reform, 1830–1841'. Other works of a general nature which may be
consulted with advantage for interpretations of developments in the
1830s are those by G. Kitson Clark, *The Making of Victorian England* (1962)
and *An Expanding Society. Britain, 1830–1900* (1967).

Parliamentary reform, both in terms of the background to the years
1830–32 and of these years themselves, is fully dealt with by J. R. M.
Butler, *The Passing of the Great Reform Bill* (1914, new impression, 1964).
The principles of the Reform Bill are lucidly summarised by N. Gash,
Politics in the Age of Peel (1953); and D. Southgate, *The Passing of the
Whigs, 1832–1886* (1962) is also helpful in this connection. External
pressures on the Whig government during the Reform Bill crisis have
received attention from J. Hamburger, *James Mill and the Art of Revolution*
(New Haven, 1963), and H. Ferguson, 'The Birmingham Political Union
and the Government' in *Victorian Studies*, III, 261–76. Various inter-
pretations of the years 1830–32 are conveniently summarised by W. H.
Maehl, Jr., *The Reform Bill of 1832* (*European Problems Studies*, 1967). The
provisions of the Reform Act are to be found in C. Seymour, *Electoral
Reform in England and Wales* (New Haven, 1915).

The constitutional and political structure of England after the Reform
Act are dealt with by N. Gash, *Reaction and Reconstruction in English Politics,
1832–1852* (Oxford, 1965), and on a more technical level by the same
author, *Politics in the Age of Peel*. A useful survey is provided by H. J.
Hanham, *The Reformed Electoral System in Great Britain* (Historical Association pamphlet, G69); and the relevant sections of J. P. Mackintosh,
The British Cabinet (2nd edn., 1968) are helpful.

On the subject of reform in State and Church after 1832, the importance of municipal reform in 1835 in the development of local government
is fully examined by S. and B. Webb, *English Local Government from the
Revolution to the Municipal Corporations Act: The Manor and the Borough*, II

(1908), and also by B. Keith-Lucas, *The English Local Government Franchise. A Short History* (Oxford, 1952). A. Briggs, *Victorian Cities* (1963) provides a most useful survey, and H. J. Dyos (ed.), *The Study of Urban History* (1968), contains much interesting and new material. Corporation reform is seen more from a contemporary political point of view by G. B. A. M. Finlayson, 'The Municipal Corporation Commission and Report, 1833–35' in *Bulletin of the Institute of Historical Research*, xxxvi, 36–52 and 'The Politics of Municipal Reform, 1835' in *English Historical Review*, LXXXI, 673–92. Church reform and the position of the dissenters in the 1830s are examined by N. Gash, *Reaction and Reconstruction*; and other works which deal with these subjects are O. Chadwick, *The Victorian Church* (1966), and G. F. A. Best, *Temporal Pillars; Queen Anne's Bounty, the Ecclesiastical Commissioners and the Church of England* (1964).

On the politics and parties of the decade after the Reform Act, N. Gash, *Reaction and Reconstruction* has chapters on both Whigs and Tories, and is especially strong on the latter; and also on this subject, G. Kitson Clark, *Peel and the Conservative Party. A Study in Party Politics, 1832–1841* (2nd edn., 1964) has much good material. The Whigs in the same period still await a detailed history; the relevant chapter of D. Southgate, *The Passing of the Whigs* is, however, a helpful guide.

The social legislation of the 1830s receives attention from D. Roberts, *Victorian Origins of the British Welfare State* (New Haven, 1960) and M. Bruce, *The Coming of the Welfare State* (1961). Factory reform is dealt with by J. T. Ward, *The Factory Movement, 1830–1855* (1962), and especially helpful is C. Driver, *Tory Radical, The Life of Richard Oastler* (New York, 1946). Both these books are valuable for the 'unofficial' movement for reform; this is also mentioned by M. W. Thomas, *The Early Factory Legislation* (1948), but this work is primarily concerned with the 'official' aspect of the question, and contains a great deal of useful material, if of a rather technical nature. On the poor law, a good survey is given by J. J. and A. J. Bagley, *The English Poor Law* (1966), and the volumes by S. and B. Webb, *English Poor Law History*, Part I, *The Old Poor Law* (1927) and Part II, *The Last Hundred Years*, (1929) contain a vast amount of information. The orthodox criticisms of the unreformed poor law are challenged by M. Blaug, 'The Myth of the Old Poor Law and the Making of the New' in *Journal of Economic History* XXIII, 151–84, and 'The Poor Law Report Re-examined' in *ibid.*, XXIV, 229–45. A very convenient summary of this reappraisal and other points are contained in J. D. Marshall, *The Old Poor Law, 1795–1834* (*Studies in Economic History*, 1968).

On the wider question of growth in government, D. Roberts, *Victorian Origins* provides a clear survey. Certain biographies, such as S. E. Finer, *Life and Times of Sir Edwin Chadwick* (1952) and R. Lambert, *Sir John Simon, 1816–1904 and English Social Administration* (1963) are also useful in this respect. A. V. Dicey, *Lectures on the Relation between Law and Public*

Opinion in England during the Nineteenth Century (2nd edn., 1914) is the starting point for much later work on this subject; his views have been subjected to re-interpretation in a number of articles which have been cited in
the text; and a useful summary of these with certain additional points is
given by V. Cromwell, 'Interpretations of Nineteenth Century Administration: an Analysis' in *Victorian Studies*, IX, 245–54, and by W. O.
Aydelotte, 'The Conservative and Radical Interpretations of Early
Victorian Social Legislation' in *Victorian Studies*, XI, 225–36.

The radical movements of the 1830s have to be traced through a
variety of works. Some of these, such as A. L. Morton and G. Tate,
The British Labour Movement, 1770–1920, a History (1956) – have to be
treated with great care owing to the political or ideological commitment
of their authors. E. P. Thompson, *The Making of the English Working
Class* (1963, Pelican edn., 1968) is a very much more sophisticated work
than that of Morton and Tate, and is immensely rich in material; but his
views on 'class' would not command universal acceptance, although
Thompson is largely unrepentant on this score, as is to be seen in the
'Postscript' to the Pelican edition of his book. S. Maccoby, *English
Radicalism, 1832–1852* (1935) contains rather scattered information, some
of which is relevant to the 1830s; J. Derry, *The Radical Tradition* (1967)
and D. Read, *The English Provinces, c. 1760–1960. A Study in Influence* (1964)
may also be consulted in this connection. D. Read, *Press and People,
1790–1850, Opinion in Three English Cities* (1961) gives a survey of many of
the radical and reform movements and summaries of the views of many
important provincial newspapers, although not all of these were in the
reform interest. The literature on Chartism is considerable; and it may
suffice to mention A. Briggs (ed.), *Chartist Studies* (1959), which examines
Chartism by locality, and also contains good general chapters; and
F. C. Mather, *Chartism* (Historical Association Pamphlet, G61) which
takes account of recent writing on the subject and provides a very clear
and concise survey of various aspects of the movement. The Anti-Corn
Law League is very well analysed by N. McCord in his book of that title
(1958). The parliamentary radicals may be studied through various
biographies, such as G. Wallas, *Life of Francis Place* (rev. edn., 1918) and
J. K. Buckley, *Joseph Parkes of Birmingham* (1926). The group as a whole
are examined by J. Hamburger, *Intellectuals in Politics, John Stuart Mill and
the Philosophic Radicals* (New Haven, 1965).

There are various collections of documents which may be used in con-
nection with the period. These are, for example, those to be found in
G. M. Young and W. D. Handcock (eds.) *English Historical Documents*,
XII(I), 1833–1874 (1956). Other collections are those edited by N. Gash,
The Age of Peel (1968); by E. C. Midwinter, *Victorian Social Reform* (1968);
and G. D. H. Cole and A. W. Filson, *British Working Class Movements,
Selected Documents, 1789–1875* (1951, Paperback edn., 1965). W. Lovett,
Life and Struggles in Pursuit of Bread, Knowledge and Freedom (1876, new

edn., 1967) throws a great deal of light on working class radical movements in the decade; and F. Engels, *Condition of the Working Class in England* (German first edn., 1845. Trans. and ed. by W. O. Henderson and W. H. Chaloner, Oxford, 1958) provides a commentary on the legislation of the 1830s, written from a very 'slanted' political point of view. Finally, John Stuart Mill, *Autobiography* (1873) provides a very valuable source for a study of the parliamentary radicals in the decade.

Index

Albert, Prince, 22

Althorp, Viscount (3rd Earl Spencer), 20, 25, 46, 58, 78

Anti-Corn Law Association, 93

Anti-Corn Law League, vi, 3, 90, 93–104, 107

Anti-Poor Law Movement, 79, 82, 92, 95

Anti-Slavery Movement, 38

Ashley, Lord (7th Earl of Shaftesbury), 41, 44, 45, 46, 49, 50, 77

Association of Working Men to Procure a Cheap and Honest Press, 91

Attwood, Thomas, 7, 91, 94

Bagehot, Walter, quoted, 18

Baines, Edward, 81

Bedchamber Incident, 21

Bentham, Jeremy, 6, 43, 68, 69, 72

Benthamism, 42, 65, 66, 68, 69, 71, 72

Birmingham, 6, 7, 15, 91, 92

Birmingham Political Union, 7, 12, 13, 91, 95

Blackburne, John, 25

Blomfield, Bishop, 54

Bonham, F. R., 19

Borough representation after 1832, 14–16

Bradford, 38

Bramber, 15

Brebner, J. B., work cited, 66, 68, 69

Bristol, 12

British and Foreign Schools Society, 65

Brotherton, Joseph, 47

Buckingham and Chandos, 3rd Duke of, 28

Bull, Rev. George S., 41

Burn, W. L., work cited, 67

Cambridge, University of, 16

Carlton Club, 19

Catholic Emancipation, 8

Chadwick, Edwin, 42, 46, 54, 68

'Chandos Clause', 17

Chartism, vi, 90–105, 107

Church of England, 1, 2, 23, 24, 31, 32, 33

Church Rates, 32, 33, 94

Church Rates Abolition Society, 94

Clark, G. Kitson, work cited, 67, 69

Class and class consciousness, consideration of, 97–100, 102

Cleve, John, 76

Cobbett, William, 54

Cobden, Richard, 83, 93, 96, 101

Commons, House of, see Parliament

Conservative party and Conservatism, see Tories

Co-operative movement, 73, 74, 79, 80

Corn Laws, 83, 84, 90, 93, 95, 98, 100, 101, 102, 104

Cotton Spinners Union, 74

County representation after 1832, 16, 17

Crown, see Parliament

Derby, 12, 76

Dicey, A. V., work cited, vi, 65–7

Dissent and Dissenters, 2, 24, 32–3, 36, 94, 106

Dorchester, 81

Durham, 1st Earl of, 10, 85, 88

East Retford, 6

Ecclesiastical Commission (1836), 1, 32

Education, 65, 70

Eliot, Ebenezer, quoted, 84

Established Church Act (1836), 31

Evangelical Toryism, 37, 38, 39, 72

Factory Acts: (1831), 37, 38, 45; (1833), v, 3, 37, 46–50, 69–70, 71, 72, 78, 79, 82, 85, 106

Finsbury, 15
Fixby, 38
Free Trade, 34, 104
Friendly Society of Agricultural Labourers, 81

General Elections: (1830), 9; (1831), 11; (1832), 19, 34, 35, 40, 86; (1835), 20, 34, 35, 36; (1837), 20, 34, 36, 89; (1841), 21, 36
George IV, 9, 10
Glasgow, 84
Grampound, 8
Grand National Consolidated Trades Union, 80, 81
Grand National Moral Union of the Productive Classes of the United Kingdom, 79–80
Grey, 2nd Earl, 9, 10, 11, 12, 13, 19
Grote, George, 87
Grote, Mrs., 103

Harney, George, 76, 79
Hart, Mrs. J., work cited, 69
Hetherington, Henry, 73, 76, 91, 93, 102
Hindley, Charles, 47
Hobhouse, Sir J. C., 37, 38, 39, 40
Huddersfield, 25, 38, 79
Hume, Joseph, 84

Ireland, 34, 104

Jamaica, suspension of constitution, 21

Keith-Lucas, B., work cited, 29–30

Laissez faire, 65, 66, 67, 69, 70, 71, 106
Lambert, R., work cited, 68
Lancashire, 40, 41, 81, 84
Leeds, 7, 8, 15, 39, 40, 81, 93
Leeds Mercury, 38, 81, 82, 83, 84
Leicester, 30
Liberal Toryism, 8
Liverpool, 7, 84
London, 14, 15, 40, 73, 75, 76, 84, 91
London, University of, 33
London Working Men's Association, 90, 91, 92, 97, 98

Londonderry, 3rd Marquis of, 28
Lords, House of, *see* Parliament
Lovett, William, 91, 93, 96
Lyndhurst, Lord, 27, 76

McCord, N., work cited, 94
MacDonagh, O., work cited, 69
Malthus, T. R., 53
Manchester, 6, 7, 15, 29, 31, 40, 81, 83, 84, 90, 93, 101
Manchester Guardian, 81, 82
Melbourne, Viscount, 19, 20, 21, 81, 84
Mill, James, 6
Mill, John Stuart, 102
Molesworth, Sir William, 89
Municipal Corporations, 23, 24, 25, 87
Municipal Corporations Act (1835), v, vi, 1, 29–31, 33, 75, 81, 83, 84, 85, 86, 87, 88, 89, 106
Municipal Corporations Bill (1835), 26–9, 33, 34, 85

National Association for the Protection of Labour, 74
National Political Union, 12
National Society, 65
National Union of the Working Classes, 7, 73, 74, 75, 76, 91
Newcastle, 7
New Lanark, 54
Newspaper Stamp Duty, 73, 76–7, 86, 91
Northern Star, 77, 92
Nottingham, 12, 60

Oastler, Richard, 38, 39, 41, 77, 79, 82, 92
O'Brien, Bronterre, 97, 102
O'Connor, Feargus, 92, 96, 102
Old Sarum, 15
Owen, Robert, 54, 74, 79, 80

Paine, Thomas, 5
Parkes, Joseph, 8, 12, 25, 26, 85, 86, 87, 88, 89, 101–2
Parliament, Crown, v, 2, 10–13, 18–22; House of Lords, v, 2, 10–14, 22, 27–8; House of Commons, v, 2, 10–12, 22–3

Parris, H., work cited, 67, 69

Party, divisions and organisation, 2, 19, 20, 21, 22, 23, 33, 36, 106

Patten, Wilson, 41–2

Peel, Sir Robert, 13, 20, 21, 22, 26–7, 28–9, 31, 32, 34, 35, 36, 101, 104, 105, 106–7

Penryn, 6

Place, Francis, 8, 12, 85, 88, 89, 98, 100, 101, 102

Plympton, 15

Political Unions, 10, 13, 73

Poor Law Amendment Act (1834), v, 3, 58–62, 72, 78, 82, 92, 95, 101, 104, 106

Poor Man's Guardian, 73, 76, 79, 80

Population, 18

Potter, Thomas, 93

Prisons Act (1835), 64–5

Prouty, R., work cited, 66, 69

Radicalism, working class, 5–7, 73–81, 90–1; middle class, 5–7, 73, 81–4, 90; parliamentary, 6, 73, 84–90, 100–2, 107

Railway Act (1840), 65

Reform Act (1832), v, 2, 14–23, 74–5, 76, 83, 84, 86, 87, 91, 93, 105

Reform Bills (1831–32), 10–14, 33, 85, 91

Reform Club, 19

Register of births, marriages and deaths, 32, 106

Religious Freedom Society, 94

Ricardo, David, 53, 54

Ripon, 31

Roberts, D., work cited, 61, 62, 63, 66–7, 68, 69

Roebuck, J. A., 85, 86, 87

Royal Commissions, 71; on Factories (1833), 37, 41, 42, 43, 44, 45, 46, 72, 77, 78; on Municipal Corporations (1835), 25–6, 35, 87; on Poor Laws (1834), 54–8, 64, 70, 72

Russell, Lord John, 1st Earl Russell, 6, 8, 10, 12, 20, 26, 33, 34, 89

Sadler, Michael, 39, 40, 41, 45, 77

Select Committees, 71; on Factories (1832), 37, 40, 41, 77; (1840), 49, 50; on Municipal Corporations (1833), 25

Senior, Nassau, 54

Short Time Committees, 37, 39, 40, 74, 77, 79

Slavery, abolition of, 4

Smith, J. E., 80

Smith, Southwood, 42

Speenhamland system, 52–3, 54, 55

Stephen, J. R., 102

Tamworth Manifesto, 35, 106

Ten Hour Bill (1833), 39, 40, 41, 44, 45, 46, 77, 78

Ten Hour Movement, 37, 39, 40, 41, 42, 43, 44, 47, 72, 78, 91

Thomson, Poulett, 47, 84

Thompson, E. P., work cited, 99

Tithes, 33

Tolpuddle Martyrs, 81, 93

Tories, 2, 8, 11, 13, 14, 19, 20, 21, 33, 86, 87, 88, 102; and development of Conservative party and Conservatism, 35–6, 104–5

Tower Hamlets, 15

Trade Union Movement, 73, 74, 79, 80, 81, 90, 91, 93, 95, 97, 98

United Committee of Dissenters, 32

University College, London, 33

Victoria, Queen, 20, 21, 22

Watson, James, 76

Wellington, Duke of, 8, 9, 13

Whigs, 2, 6, 9–14, 19, 20, 21, 25–6, 28, 29, 31–2, 32–3, 34, 36, 49, 54, 65, 75, 77, 78, 79, 84, 86, 87, 88, 89, 90, 102–3

William IV, 10–11, 12, 13, 19, 20, 21, 28

Wilson, George, 93, 96

Wilson, John, 42

Wood, John, 38

Yorkshire, 8, 37, 39, 41, 84